NEO-ASTROLOGY

Michel Gauquelin was born in Paris in 1928. He is considered one of the most controversial but also celebrated researchers into astrology. He began his researches very young, in the late forties, and from then on spent his life assessing evidence for or against cosmic influence. He studied psychology and statistics at the Sorbonne. His first book, *The Influence of the Stars: A Critical and Empirical Study*, published in 1955 in Paris, aroused considerable interest. It was in this book that he published his theory of the 'Mars effect' on sports champions and many other ideas on relationships between birthtimes, planets and careers. Later, he demonstrated the strong links between planets and personality and the role of heredity in them.

From 1969 until his death in 1991, he was the director of the Laboratoire d'Étude des Relations entre Rythmes Cosmiques et Psychophysiologiques (LERRCP), based in Paris. He wrote more than twenty books on psychology and astrology, which have been translated into several languages. These include *The Scientific Basis of Astrology* (1970), *The Cosmic Clocks* (1982), *Cosmic Influences on Human Behaviour* (1983), *The Truth About Astrology* (1983), *The Spheres of Destiny: Your Personality and the Planets* (1984) and *Written in the Stars* (1988). He was also the editor of a series of books devoted to psychology and scientific consultant of the French magazine *Psychologie*. In 1969 he was awarded a medal for psychological writings from the 16th Congress of Health, Ferrara, Italy.

NEO-ASTROLOGY:
A COPERNICAN REVOLUTION

MICHEL GAUQUELIN

TRANSLATED BY STELA TOMAŠEVIĆ

ARKANA

ARKANA

Published by the Penguin Group
27 Wrights Lane, London W8 5TZ, England
Penguin Books USA Inc., 375 Hudson Street, New York 10014, USA
Penguin Books Australia Ltd, Ringwood, Victoria, Australia
Penguin Books Canada Ltd, 10 Alcorn Avenue, Toronto, Ontario, Canada M4V 3B2
Penguin Books (NZ) Ltd, 182–190 Wairau Road, Auckland 10, New Zealand

Penguin Books Ltd, Registered Offices: Harmondsworth, Middlesex, England

First published by Penguin 1991
1 3 5 7 9 10 8 6 4 2

Copyright © The Estate of Michel Gauquelin, 1991
Translation copyright © Stela Tomašević, 1991
All rights reserved

The moral rights of the author and of the translator have been asserted

The author and publishers wish to thank Éditions Traditionnelles
(previously Chacornac) for permission to reproduce and quote from
Langage astral and *Essai de psychologie astrale*, by Paul Choisnard

Printed in England by Clays Ltd, St Ives plc
Set in 10/12½ pt Monophoto Photina

Except in the United States of America, this book is sold subject
to the condition that it shall not, by way of trade or otherwise, be lent,
re-sold, hired out, or otherwise circulated without the publisher's
prior consent in any form of binding or cover other than that in
which is is published and without a similar condition including this
condition being imposed on the subsequent purchaser

*To all my friends of Fresno, California,
where this book was written*

'I want to be smart'

Charlie, in *Flowers for Algernon*
by Daniel Keyes

CONTENTS

List of Illustrations ... xi
Preface: From Cosmic Clocks to Neo-Astrology ... 1
Lifting the Curtain: Astrology as Universal Law ... 4

ACT ONE:
Cast of Characters

1 The Horoscope in a Nutshell ... 13
2 The Gauquelin Results ... 21
3 Science and the Mars Effect ... 32

First Interlude: In Search of a Lost Paradigm ... 41

ACT TWO:
The Babylonians

4 On the Way to the Horoscope ... 49
5 An Early 'Grain of Gold'? ... 55

ACT THREE:
Greek Astrology

6 The Four Pillars of the Sky ... 67
7 Astral Psychology ... 78

Second Interlude: Kepler: Astronomer, Astrologer ... 87

Contents

ACT FOUR:
The Renaissance

8	The Last Magicians	99
9	Saturn and Melancholy	116
10	Children of the Planets	128

ACT FIVE:
The Twentieth Century

11	The Trojan Horse	140
12	Unfortunate Forerunners	151

Epilogue: From the Harmony of the Spheres to Chaos 167

Notes 179

LIST OF ILLUSTRATIONS

Figure 1: A birthchart   14

Figure 2: Gauquelin's 'plus zones' v. horoscope houses   27

Figure 3: A neo-astrological interpretation   30

Figure 4: The Mars effect and sports champions   37
Sources: M. Gauquelin, *Les hommes et les astres*, Denoël (Paris 1960); *Journal of Interdisciplinary Cycle*, 3 (1972); and Comité Para in *Nouvelles Brèves*, 43 (1976).

Figure 5: The four angles of the Greek horoscope (A.D. 15)   71
Source: O. Neugebauer and H. B. Hoesen, *Greek Horoscopes*, The American Philosophical Society (Philadelphia 1959), p. 18.

Figure 6: The four angles of the Greek horoscope (A.D. 497)   72
Source: O. Neugbauer and H. B. Hoesen, *Greek Horoscopes*, The American Philosophical Society (Philadelphia 1959), p. 156.

Figure 7: Horoscope of the Roman Emperor Hadrian   85
Source: Modern representation modified according to O. Neugebauer and H. B. Van Hoesen, *Greek Horoscopes*, The American Philosophical Society (Philadelphia 1959), pp. 90 and 220.

Figure 8a: Robert Burton's horoscope   118
Source: J. C. Eade, *The Forgotten Sky*, Oxford University Press (New York, 1984), p. 53.

Figure 8b: Robert Burton's horoscope: A modern graphic
representation 119

Figure 9: *Melencolia I*, by Albrecht Dürer 122

Figure 10: The rise and fall of astrology 142
Source: Adapted from M. Graubard, *Astrology and Alchemy, Two Fossil Sciences*, Philosophical Library (New York 1953), p. 233.

Figure 11: Planetary intensity in the houses according to Choisnard 156
Source: P. Choisnard, *Langage astral*, Chacornac (Paris 1940), p. 116.

Figure 12: The twelve houses according to Lasson 164
Source: *Ceux qui nous guident*, Debresse (Paris 1946), p. 148.

Figure 13: Tibetan Mandala and the planetary effect in the Gauquelin 'plus zones' 177

Table 1: The planets of success in different professional groups 25
Source: M. Gauquelin, *Les hommes et les astres*, Denoël (Paris 1960), p. 200.

Table 2: Extract of twenty traits describing planetary types 29
Source: M. Gauquelin, *The Truth about Astrology*, Blackwell (Oxford 1983), p. 70.

Preface

FROM COSMIC CLOCKS TO NEO-ASTROLOGY

As the saying goes, 'Only a fool never changes his mind.' The present work is the product of the evolution of my ideas since the publication, over twenty years ago, of my book *The Cosmic Clocks*. When it appeared, in 1967, *The Cosmic Clocks* was considered an important work. This is probably because it presented, for the first time, scientific discoveries which showed the reality of many connections, previously unknown, between man and the cosmos.

However, *The Cosmic Clocks* was the profession of faith of a *new* science of cosmic influences; resolutely forward-looking, it rejected anything that might demonstrate – even tentatively – that there was some truth to astrology. The author of the preface, the biologist Professor Frank A. Brown, stated with conviction: 'Man is unquestionably and inextricably linked by many threads with the rest of the universe, not only by way of the physical instruments he has invented and constructed, but also by way of the amazing sensitivities of his own living substance.'[1] But these links were not for him of an astrological nature, even if they appeared to be.

My rather Manichean theory was that astrology had *at best* only an intuition of the subtle connections just discovered by researchers and about to revolutionize science. Out of this came the subtitle 'From Astrology to a Modern Science'.

None of the work of Brown, Piccardi, Takata and Chizhevsky that I presented, although avant-garde, stemmed from the astrological tradition. And, although they were criticized by their conservative colleagues for being too open to new ideas, these researchers were not astrologers. In fact, they found being called 'defenders of astrology' quite an embarrassment. After my editor suggested that the subtitle for *The Cosmic Clocks* should be 'The New Implications of Astrology', Frank Brown reacted violently, threatening to withdraw his preface!

Chapter 11, 'Planets and Heredity', in which I summarized my observations, was rather like a duckling born in the midst of a brood of chicks. While Piccardi spoke of the influence of sunspots on chemical reactions, while Brown emphasized the biological role of the earth's magnetic field on human beings, I boldly described the relationship between the time of birth, the position of the planets, professional success and heredity. Was it not ungrateful simply to label my conclusions 'new science'? My work had an astrological feel to it as everyone correctly appreciated.

Another anecdote on the subject of *The Cosmic Clocks* deserves a mention here. As I had abundantly cited their compatriot, the pioneer Chizhevsky, on the relationship between sunspots and the human factor, the Russians were flattered. Moreover, my timing was right. Chizhevsky had just died, rehabilitated, after having been deported to Siberia for several years: he had been imprudent enough to attribute social revolutions to solar activity rather than to the struggle of the working classes against the bourgeoisie. Some Russian friends informed me that my book had just been translated by a Leningrad publisher and that the date of publication was officially set for April 1969. I was delighted that, in this way, my ideas would be disseminated in the Soviet Union. However, the work never appeared in print.

I found out what was at the bottom of this when I went to Leningrad myself two years later to meet a publisher who was rather reluctant to receive me. In an English that was possibly deliberately unintelligible, he told me that publication had been stopped at the last moment by the censor, precisely because of chapter 11, which was regarded as too astrological, and even occult. It was suggested that if I agreed to withdraw it, it might be possible to publish the book in the Soviet Union. I refused.

In fact, the main purpose of *The Cosmic Clocks* was indeed to present my bizarre results within the framework of the new science that I was championing. However, the righteous indignation that had made me reject any astrological context for my work, had also caused me, more or less unconsciously, to close my eyes to the evidence. In the end, this proved to be a political error, a fact that the men of science left me in no doubt about when they awarded me the derisive title of 'neo-astrologer'. In any case, I never forgot the lesson.

Those who have wished to follow the evolution of my work, its impact on the scientific community and the controversies it has aroused since the publication of *The Cosmic Clocks* know that I now accept the title of neo-astrologer, and even revel in it.

I took the first step towards becoming a neo-astrologer in 1973, when I maintained, in *Cosmic Influences on Human Behavior*,[2] that there was 'a grain of gold' in astrology. However, it is only quite recently that I began seeking to understand the whys and wherefores of this 'grain of gold' – its origins; how it had reached us after great vicissitudes; and the deep scientific implications of its reality. In *The Truth about Astrology* in 1983, I resolutely maintained:

> The observations of planetary effects at birth would demonstrate that the age-old, good-for-nothing, fossilized astrology was not pure legend after all. And that is the source of opposition to my work – the fear that an 'astrological' Copernican revolution would destroy a particular vision of the universe and shatter belief in a scientific creed which has excluded 'neo-astrology', just as it ignored the intuition of the Chaldean priest.[3]

'An "astrological" Copernican revolution' may sound rather pompous: it is about time I proved that it is, in fact, a reality.

Lifting the Curtain

ASTROLOGY AS UNIVERSAL LAW

On 30 December 1954, during the annual meeting of the History of Science Society, the famous science historian, Lynn Thorndike, read a paper entitled: 'The True Place of Astrology in the History of Science', which caused quite a sensation. This is how it began:

> The true place of astrology in the history of science is a vast subject with countless ramifications which it would take a long time to pursue and many pages to relate. My present purpose is to emphasize a single point, but one which is the most important and fundamental of all. Briefly stated, it is that, during the long period of scientific development before Sir Isaac Newton promulgated the universal law of gravitation, there had been generally recognized and accepted another and different universal natural law, which his supplanted. And that universal law was astrological.
>
> This general law that the world of nature and of life on this earth is governed by the movements of the stars is expressly repeated again and again and its truth is assumed even oftener ... to hold that natural or physical law was a concept then first inaugurated, is to do astrology a grave injustice ... Surely astrology had for centuries before believed in universal laws which govern particular events, and that nature as a whole was subject to immutable laws. Modern historians of science have been strangely blind to the fundamental and universal importance of this sweeping, all-inclusive hypothesis, that all operations of the inferior world of nature spring from and are controlled by the eternal movement of the incorruptible celestial bodies. Strangely blind also to its supreme significance in the appreciation and comprehension and evaluation of pre-Newtonian scientific thought and activity![1]

Quoting another science historian, Herbert Dingle: 'It is reasonable to look forward to the time when all the sciences will be fused into a single science, using a single set of concepts, though that time may yet be distant',[2] Thorndike retorted with this bold assertion: 'If we may look forward to such a unified science, we may also look backward to it, before the seventeenth century, to the time when all change and all phenomena in the elementary world were believed to be governed by radiations of the eternal and incorruptible, yet moving, celestial spheres.[3]

To be sure, he hastily added that he did not believe in the methods of astrology. But it is the great merit of this eminent man that he gave astrology its 'true place in the history of science', a place previously denied by many authors, who have treated astrology only as a pure superstition.

Although I pay tribute to Thorndike, I do not follow him in his refusal to believe in the possible grain of truth in astrology. For me, this grain does exist, I have discovered it or, perhaps, simply rediscovered it. But given that it exists, where has it come from? Let us reverse the time-machine to way back in the past. Let us stop it at the dawn of civilization. The stars were then gods. As Mircea Eliade puts it:

> Simple contemplation of the celestial vault suffices to provoke a religious experience. The sky shows itself to be infinite, transcendent ... Transcendence is revealed by simple awareness of infinite height. 'Most high' spontaneously becomes an attribute of divinity. The higher regions inaccessible to man, the sidereal zones, acquire the momentousness of the transcendent, of absolute reality, or eternity ... The cosmic rhythms manifest order, harmony, permanence, fecundity. The cosmos as a whole is an organism at once *real, living,* and *sacred* ...[4]

And the historian Franz Boll observes: 'As early as Sumerian times the symbol of divinity in cuneiform writing was represented by a star.'[5]

Astrology is without a doubt the first 'natural' religion of man, who soon noted the surprising links which united life on earth with the movement of the great stars, the Moon and the Sun. To the naked eye, the Sun and the Moon, equal in influence, mysteriously cover the same area in the sky.

Neo-Astrology

The prayers that man has addressed to the Sun over the centuries are innumerable. Among the most famous is the one written by Pharaoh Amenhotep IV, who ruled Egypt from 1379 to 1362 B.C. (Amenhotep IV, the mystical pharaoh, tried to replace the worship of Egyptian deities by that of a single god, Aton, the Sun-god, and adopted the name of Akhenaton in honour of that cosmic divinity.) His subjects would sing it at sunrise, and it began as follows:

> You appear in your loveliness on the horizon
> Living Sun who are as old as life
> You are on the Eastern horizon and have filled all lands
> With your beauty
> Your rays clasp the lands as far as the end
> Of all you have created.[6]

The 'birth' of the Sun every morning has always been welcomed with joy, just as there used to be magic rituals at its 'death', every night, so that the Sun-god would come to life again next morning. Even in religions as developed as Islam or Judaism, it remains obligatory to this day to pray facing the Sun at dawn.

As for the Moon-god, he ruled the souls of oriental people for thousands of years. The first inhabitants of Mesopotamia (now Iraq) called him Sin. Sin is the god of the city of Ur, the god in the sacred boat. According to Maurice Lambert:

> The boat is the crescent that drifts from one end of the sky to the other; it is the sailing boat in which the god of Ur wanders all night above the desert ... In his vessel the Moon-god drifted on the waves of darkness, just above the top of the gigantic many-storeyed tower, this landing stage for divine visitors.[7]

To this ethereal residence rose a litany of hymns, such as the following, which was addressed to the Moon-god:

> Sacred boat in the sky, self-generating greatness
> Father Moon-god, ruler of the city Ur,
> When you sail, Lord, who may surpass you, or even equal you?
> Who may adequately celebrate your journey?
> When your name spreads across the marshes, they moan;
> Let it spread over Euphrates and Tigris,
> And, day and night, the high waters become calm.[8]

Lifting the Curtain

But the Moon-god's role goes beyond just mooring at the celestial landing-stage – the man-built ziggurat. Quite early on, a visual link appeared between the crescent of the Moon and the horns of the Bull. The head of a heifer or a bull-calf found on the outskirts of Ur displays a crescent Moon as a symbol of prosperity. A more detailed description can be found in one of the hymns:

> His night is a bright lazuli,
> The whiteness of the Cow, rising moonlight.[9]

Among the influences subsequently attributed to the Moon, the Boat-Moon-Bull theme is without doubt the oldest. It is worth noting that even today in horoscopes the Moon is said to be 'strong' when passing through the sign of Taurus. With the passage of time, however, the symbolism of lunar influences was to multiply. The god favouring fertile unions and sexual compatibility among the Sumerians was to exercise the influence in various directions.

'It was lunar symbolism,' writes Mircea Eliade, 'that enabled man to relate and connect such heterogeneous things as: birth, becoming, death, and resurrection; the waters, plants, woman, fecundity and immortality; the cosmic darkness, prenatal existence, and life after death . . .'[10]

After the Moon and the Sun, the most beautiful celestial object that we can observe is the planet Venus. It soon became important for the Sumerians: Inanna (Ishtar), the planet Venus, was the daughter of the Moon-god. To quote Lambert again: 'A visible link connects it with the Moon-god, for we can often see the planet shining as night falls, solitary, a little way from the crescent Moon. She seems to be receiving orders from the Moon, to be linked to him by strong chains.'[11]

We can see rising from the dawn of Sumerian civilization, the symbol of Venus, the Babylonian Ishtar, the goddess of love. Lambert continues: 'Like her father, the Moon-god, she is full of *hi-li*;* she attracts and, through her beauty, her great wealth and her

---

* *Hi-li* is a supernatural power that is always present and always hidden.

opulence, she inspires love. Without her all desire goes. Over the centuries, however, this quality will be over-emphasized and man's adulation will pervert her. The stern Moon-god's degenerate daughter will eventually become a goddess of love.'[12]

The triad of Ur – Sin, the Moon-god, Shamash, the Sun-god his son, and Inanna, the goddess Venus his daughter – is at the origin of all astrology; it is a 'holy trinity' of sacred origin. Of course, we are still at this point a long way from the horoscope. But already we see emerging, here and there, the embryo of the famous doctrine: the importance of rising with the Sun; the fecund Moon and the sign of Taurus; Venus, the goddess (but not yet the planet) of love. As a neo-astrologer, I must admit that I have not encountered among the Sumerians the grain of astrological truth that I am looking for, even though I share their awe at the sight of the path followed by these majestic planets. But its phantom will emerge from this sacred mist, a necessary stage.

After the Sumerian era, great importance was attributed to the 'four quarters of the sky', which might with reason be connected with what will become known as the four 'angles' of the horoscope, and also with the four frontiers from which spread the 'Gauquelin zones' of neo-astrology. This is, I believe, a significant analogy. Let me quote the historian Ernest Zinner:

> When men observed the daily course of the sun along the sky they saw it rising in the East, bringing light and warmth. They found the warmth growing until the sun reached its culmination point in the South, and felt it diminishing until the sun set in the West. In other words, they observed a great system: the awakening of life in the East, its climax in the South, and its disappearance in the West. This gave them the significance of three great quarters. The North provided the fourth – the region where the sun was never seen. On the other hand, the stars were observed there at night; and the stars were always present. The North, too, was therefore an important quarter of sky and earth.[13]

In the first century A.D., the Roman Manilius adopted the idea of 'the four pillars of heaven' when he described the Greek tradition of astrology in his *Astronomicon*. But, already in the age of pyramids, the importance of the four quarters could be noted:

> Life and death, the strength of life and eternal rest, these were appropriate to the four quarters, and a wise man would follow their ruling. Hence the grandiose manner in which the Egyptians observed the four quarters. Special attention was paid to the four quarters in the construction of the great pyramids, about 2800 B.C. The Great Pyramid of Cheops, despite its size, is oriented so exactly that its edges diverge from the main points by no more than three minutes.[14]

When Pharaoh Seti I built a temple in 1300 B.C., he had engraved on it the following inscription in which the goddess of wisdom speaks to him: 'The hammer in my hand was of gold when I hammered the peg, and it was you who held the cord. Your hand held the spade when its corners were fixed with the four pillars of heaven.'[15]

ACT ONE

Cast of Characters

1

THE HOROSCOPE IN A NUTSHELL

We have undertaken this brief journey into the past, to the age of the Sumerians and the great pyramids, so that we can grasp the idea of astrology at its source. We need, though, to return to the present, to A.D. 1990, that is, some 5,000 years on. For a full understanding and in the interest of the thesis defended in this book, it is essential to give a summary of the horoscopic rules in use today. Readers whose only knowledge of astrology is based on what they see in the daily papers will be grateful to me for the next few pages. Specialists will forgive me, I hope, for briefly listing ideas that are familiar to them.

What is astrology? It is the art – or science, opinions differ on this point – of describing the character or destiny of a person by observing the position of the stars at the moment of the person's birth. This needs further explanation.

Figure 1 is the representation of a finished horoscope, also called a birthchart (the author's). It is easy to read for those who know the language of the stars; but is indecipherable for those who don't, who represent the majority. For the latter, it will be useful to describe, in brief, the astrologer's sky, that is, what the horoscope corresponds to astronomically.

THE ASTRONOMICAL SETTING

The astronomical universe of an astrologer is limited to the solar system, the Moon and the planets. It is a world of appearances. What I mean by this is that the sky is seen as if the Earth were the centre of the universe, and that the movements of the stars are

Neo-Astrology

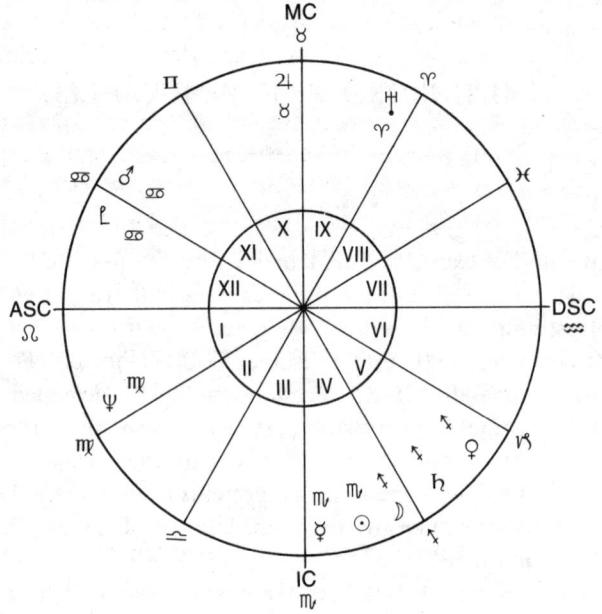

Figure 1: A birthchart.

observed as they appear to us and not as they occur from the astronomical view point. The horoscope represents the momentary position of the planets in the sky at the time of birth. It is chiefly composed of:

- twelve signs of the zodiac
- ten planets
- twelve houses
- five main aspects

The Zodiac

The Sun, the Moon and the planets follow an almost identical path across the celestial sphere. All these stars circulate within a zone which does not go beyond 8 degrees on either side of the ecliptic. The ecliptic is the great circle of the celestial sphere which the Sun travels during one year, at the rate of approximately one degree per day. This circular strip/line of 16 degrees is called the zodiac. The zodiacal band is divided by astronomers into 360 degrees. Astrologers have divided the 360 degrees into sections of 30 degrees each. These are the twelve signs of the zodiac so important in astrology: Aries, Taurus, Gemini, Cancer, Leo, Virgo, Libra, Scorpio, Sagittarius, Capricorn, Aquarius and Pisces. The Sun enters Aries, the first sign, on 21 March, that is, at the time of the spring equinox. It enters Taurus, the second sign, on 21 April, etc.

The Planets

The astrological world is composed of the ten stars of the solar system, the Sun, the Moon and the planets in order of their distance from the Sun: Mercury, Venus, Mars, Jupiter, Saturn, Uranus, Neptune and Pluto. The Sun, the lord of our system, without whom there would be no life on Earth, is familiar to all, as is our satellite, the Moon. Mercury is the smallest of the planets and the one closest to the Sun. Venus is approximately the same size as the Earth. It shines brightly as the 'morning star' when it precedes the Sun and as the 'evening star' when it follows it, and it appears at dusk. The other planets are called 'superior' as they move around the Sun at a greater distance than the Earth. The closest to us is Mars, of somewhat reddish colour and smaller than the Earth. Then comes Jupiter, the largest planet in the solar system, followed by Saturn and its rings which shines less brightly. Beyond them are Uranus, Neptune and Pluto, invisible to the naked eye and discovered in 1781, 1846 and 1930 respectively.

The Houses

To understand the astronomical significance of the houses, we must remember that the Earth takes twenty-four hours to complete a full revolution on its axis. As a result of this rotation, all the stars appear to have travelled across the celestial sphere in one day. Astrologers, struck by the alternation of day and night, regarded a day as a reduced year. And, in the same way as they divided the zodiac into twelve signs, they divided the diurnal movement of the stars into twelve parts, which they called 'houses'. In twenty-four hours, every star in the solar system crosses the twelve houses. These houses are numbered from I to XII in the opposite direction to that of the diurnal movement of the planets, the starting point being the Ascendant. Moreover, astrologers ascribe an essential role to the Ascendant, the degree of the zodiac which is rising on the horizon at the moment of birth.

The Aspects

The aspects are the angles formed by the planets as seen from the Earth, and viewed in pairs in the zodiac. Astrologers attach great importance to some of the angular degrees, and especially to 0 degree (the conjunction) to 60 degrees (the sextile); to 90 degrees (the square) to 120 degrees (the trine), or to 180 degrees (the opposition).

The Horoscope

Having set up the astronomical scene, we come to the horoscope. For a given place, date and time of birth, all the planets will have a place in a sign of the zodiac as well as in a house, and they will form among themselves specific aspects. Calculation of the elements of the sky at birth is not very complicated, but requires the use of specialized ephemerides, to which I refer the interested reader. It must also be said that today it has become very easy to calculate a horoscope for those who own a personal computer, as there are numerous programmes which give the positions of the planets almost instantaneously.

THE ASTROLOGICAL SIGNIFICANCE

Once all the components of the birthchart have been calculated and compiled the role of the astrologer is to decipher and interpret them so that a person's character or fate may be revealed. To 'do somebody's horoscope', it is important to know the *astrological* significance of the given astronomical elements.

The Signs of the Zodiac

The twelve signs are the cornerstone of astrology. They belong to a very old tradition passed down, in particular, by Manilius in the first century A.D. Manilius asserted that each sign had clearly defined characteristics, influences that were transmitted to a child at birth and that determined its character, health, and destiny. I will confine myself here to talking about character, but all three are part of astrology. In other words, each sign simultaneously influences character, health and fate.

A person is endowed by the characteristics of the signs occupied by the Sun, the Ascendant or several planets at the time of his or her birth. From this premise, twelve psychological types were evolved and, at a time when characterology as we know it did not exist, the qualities attributed to each sign served as a tentative science. The following *very briefly* lists the influences of the twelve signs of the zodiac – taken from several astrological treatises.

> *Aries*: Impatient, enthusiastic, independent, aggressive
> *Taurus*: Down-to-earth, calm, sensual, stable, faithful
> *Gemini*: Cunning, flexible, bright, superficial, witty, unstable
> *Cancer*: Imaginative, sensitive, family type, aware of the past
> *Leo*: Magnanimous, proud, individualistic, authoritarian, arrogant
> *Virgo*: Prudent, calculating, meticulous, careful

Libra: Conciliatory, sociable, refined, sense of justice
Scorpio: Critical, discerning, profound, aggressive
Sagittarius: Extrovert, generous, loyal, enjoys travel
Capricorn: Serious, calm, far-sighted, secretly ambitious
Aquarius: Enjoys novelty, original, idealistic, utopian
Pisces: Emotional, impressionable, intuitive, devoted, indecisive

The Role of the Planets

If the signs of the zodiac are the fabric, then the planets represent the embroidery. Thus the planets – including the Sun and the Moon – acquire the tonality of the sign through which they are passing, while contributing their own symbolic language. This language comes from a very ancient tradition of which traces are still found today in everyday speech. A 'lunatic', a 'Venus' for a beautiful woman, a 'martial' step, a 'jovial' laugh, 'saturnine' behaviour, these are all terms directly inspired by the influences which astrologers attribute to the Moon, Venus, Mars, Jupiter and Saturn.

While concentrating again mainly on character, the following list gives a *very brief* synthesis – also taken from various astrological treatises – of the main influences the planets may have on all of us. These are especially significant if a planet is in a 'strong' position in the horoscope, for example, if it is found in a sign which suits its nature, if it has a large number of 'aspects' with other planets, or if it occupies one of the four 'angular' houses (I, IV, VII or X) and so on.

Sun: Proud, magnanimous, powerful, generous, sometimes arrogant
Moon: Imaginative, intuitive, fickle, sociable, lazy
Mercury: Intelligent, vivacious, shrewd, opportunistic, cunning, unstable
Venus: Sensitive, calm, a lover of life in all its forms
Mars: Energetic, combative, courageous, impulsive, violent
Jupiter: Outgoing, earnest, just, vain, self-centred
Saturn: Serious, reserved, profound, egoistical, vindictive, pessimistic

Uranus: Original, independent, passionate, eccentric
Neptune: Fanciful, intuitive, fickle, prone to mysticism
Pluto: The dark side of things, immanent justice

The Role of the Aspects and the Houses

In astrology, a distinction is made between 'good' and 'bad' aspects. There are two good and two bad aspects, plus a fifth, the conjunction, which is sometimes favourable, sometimes, unfavourable. So far, so fair. The sextile (planets 60-degrees distant) and the trine (120-degrees distant) are good. The square (planets 90-degrees distant) and the opposition (180-degrees distant) are bad.

The houses, the sections of the sky which govern various areas of life, comprise a rather surprising mixture of influences. The following list provides a few key-words.

House I: the subject him/herself, character, physical appearance
House II: gains, all that is earned by the subject him/herself
House III: brothers and sisters, short journeys
House IV: father and mother, the home, the end of life
House V: pleasures, loves, entertainment, children
House VI: work, employees, small animals, acute illness
House VII: marriage, spouse, associates, enemies
House VIII: death, inheritance
House IX: long journeys, religion, philosophy
House X: occupation, success, honours
House XI: friends, social relationships
House XII: ordeals, chronic illness, prison

The Value of the Horoscope

The list above illustrates that the wealth of information presented in the horoscope may be of great value to psychology and to human destiny. However, this wealth may in itself be somewhat disturbing. Does a horoscope really have the virtues which are so generously ascribed to it? It would, of course, be very convenient to be able to say to someone: 'Give me your date of birth and I will tell you who you are and what you will be doing.' This, to my mind, deserves objective examination and it has been the focus of my work for over forty years.

Having collected half a million dates of birth from the most diverse people, I have been able to observe that the majority of the elements in a horoscope seem not to possess any of the influences which have been attributed to them. Is astrology then based on erroneous premises? Not entirely, I believe. Although there is a large percentage of errors, a small percentage of facts remains correct, as elusive as a grain of sand lost in the sand – but a grain that has germinated as a result of experience, producing a plant with many offshoots: neo-astrology, a science based essentially on what is customarily called in specialist circles the 'Gauquelin results'.

2

THE GAUQUELIN RESULTS

For the reader who is unfamiliar with my methods and results, the following summary of what are called the 'Gauquelin results' will facilitate understanding of the ensuing chapters. First of all, I shall set the astronomical scene, that is, explain what the neo-astrological area of the Gauquelin results corresponds to astronomically.[1]

THE SKY AND THE DIURNAL MOVEMENT

Let us imagine that we are in Iraq, Chaldea of the past, and that we have climbed to the top of the ziggurat of Ur, the tiered tower of the astrological priests. The tower is the only elevated point in the completely flat, yellow plain. The night is clear.[2]

While looking at the sky, we observe constellations which have familiar names, the Great Bear, the Little Bear, Draco (the Dragon), Hercules and Orion. We can also see the Moon and some planets. The planets generally appear much brighter than most of the stars, even when they are much smaller, because they are part of the solar system and are therefore much closer to us than the stars.

It is midnight and the air is clear and cool. The Moon rises on the eastern horizon. Mars is just above our heads and Jupiter is about to set in the misty western horizon. The other planets are below the horizon and therefore not visible. Four hours later, the astral configurations have changed places. The stars, the Moon and the planets have advanced in the same direction and travelled the same distance. For example, the Great Bear has moved westward, the Moon is now high in the sky, and Mars is on the point of setting. Jupiter has disappeared and continues its journey under the Earth.

Neo-Astrology

Venus has risen above the horizon, announcing the arrival of the Sun. But these movements are only apparent, the consequence of the Earth revolving on its axis in twenty-four hours of steady movement. Every day in Ur, but also in London, Paris or New York, the same phenomenon occurs in relation to all the stars. In this way the Sun, the Moon, the planets and constellations rise, reach the highest point in the sky (upper culmination), set, reach the lowest point in the sky (lower culmination), then rise again the next day. However, each star follows its own horary circle in time and space.

THE GAUQUELIN SECTORS

Astronomers have long known how to calculate when the Sun, Moon and planets will rise, culminate or set. Their calculations are published every year in the astronomical ephemeris of each country. To determine the movement of Mars seen from Paris on 24 May 1956, I may consult the French ephemeris for the year 1956. It is there that I will discover that Mars rose at 0.44 am, reached its culmination at 5.33 am and set at 10.22 am. In the same way, it is possible to determine the daily position of the Sun, the Moon and the planets with great precision whatever place and date are given.

Now, let us suppose that a child was born on 24 May 1956 in Paris. The position of Mars will vary depending on the exact time of birth. For example, if the time is 1.00 am, Mars will just be above the horizon and rising; if it is 6.00 am, Mars will just be passing its highest point of culmination. However, as I wish to apply statistical tests properly, the information I require will have to be more precise, particularly as I need to divide the circle of diurnal movement into sectors serving as points of reference.

Astrologers (see the previous chapter) also divide the circles of diurnal movement into twelve sectors which they call 'houses'. The houses are numbered anticlockwise starting with the Ascendant (rising sign), and each house is linked to an area of human life. However, at the start of my research, my goal was not purely astrological but above all statistical. It thus served my purpose, forty years ago, to divide the diurnal movement of each planet into thirty-six sectors which I numbered from 1 to 36, beginning with the Ascendant and following the astronomical movement clockwise. Similarly, I had the idea of dividing the diurnal movement by twelve or by eighteen to obtain larger sectors, the sectors obtained from the former division being quite similar – *at least astronomically* – to the twelve houses used by the astrologers.

In my system, at the time of a child's birth, the Sun, the Moon and the planets are all situated in one or other of the thirty-six sectors of the celestial circle. Thus, if I study a group of 1,000 births, I will be able to count the number of times a given planet shows up in a given sector, just as we can count, in the casinos of Las Vegas or Atlantic City, the number of times that the ball stops on the same number after we have turned the roulette wheel a thousand times.[3]

CELEBRITIES AND THE PLANETS

As early as 1951, strange results emerged from my work on the birth of people who had succeeded in their profession. My very first observation was especially striking: at the time of birth of 576 distinguished members of the French Académie de Médecine, the planets were *not* distributed at random in the sections of the diurnal movement. This observation could not be rejected as being the result of pure chance. Any statistician would have considered it very significant – as I did. The figures I obtained indicated that famous physicians showed a preference for coming into the world when Mars or Saturn appeared in the section situated just after the rise or just after the culmination. On the other hand, a group of ordinary people, picked at random from the register of births to serve as a control group, showed no such tendency.

Somewhat intrigued, I decided to do the experiment again to see whether this strange anomaly could be repeated. Again, 508 other French physicians, also well-known, showed the same inexplicable tendency: Mars and Saturn were found with an unusual frequency in the same rising and culminating sections.[4]

TIMING THE DESTINY

My first observations concerning the physicians encouraged me to assemble other data on the birth of famous people: actors, writers, sportsmen, scientists, etc. Success is not the arbitrary criterion that it may seem for an investigation: it is relatively easy for people to agree on whether a person may be regarded as successful in life or not. Success is also a convenient criterion, since information on the birth of famous people is easily accessible in bibliographical gazetteers.

Subsequent results only confirmed and amplified my initial discovery about the physicians. On the whole, it emerged that there was an increasingly solid statistical link between the time of birth of great men and their occupational success. As was the case with the physicians of the Académie de Médecine, each occupation responded to the planetary messages in its own particular way. Mars, Jupiter, Saturn and the Moon were in turn concerned.

In certain cases, the presence of a rising or culminating planet at birth seemed to be the 'cause' of success; in others the same presence seemed to 'prevent' it (the same observations apply if a planet is setting or reaching lower culmination, but less so). The effects observed were extremely improbable, much too improbable to explain away as a mere stroke of luck. The results were published in 1955 and they have been successfully repeated many times since then (details may be found in my previous books).[5] I shall confine myself here to Table 1 opposite, which summarizes my most fundamental observations. Having collected over 20,000 dates of birth of professional celebrities from various European countries and from the United States, I had to draw the unavoidable conclusion that the position of the planets at birth is linked to one's destiny. What a challenge to a rational mind!

PLANETS AND CHARACTER

Since 1955, I have put forward the hypothesis that the real correlation is not between planets and success but between planets and

Table 1: The planets of success in different professional groups.

after the rise and upper culmination of	high frequencies of births	low frequencies of births
Jupiter	actors and playwrights politicians military leaders top executives journalists	scientists physicians
Saturn	scientists physicians	actors journalists writers painters
Mars	physicians military leaders sports champions top executives	painters musicians writers
Moon	writers politicians	sports champions

traits of character.[6] For example, sports champions are regarded as energetic, courageous and aggressive. The time of their birth is linked to the position of the planet Mars. One may therefore suppose that there is a link between Mars and the traits of character that lead to success in sport.

The same hypothesis has, of course, been extended to other occupations – like acting, writing or science research – and other planets – Jupiter, Saturn, the Moon. These surprising planetary influences owe nothing to blind fate. Certain personality traits are influenced by (or associated with) planets. To test the validity of this hypothesis, in 1967 I perfected a scientific technique which I called 'the trait of character method'. Assisted by Françoise Schneider-Gauquelin, who was then my wife, and by other colleagues, I extracted the traits of character of famous people from thousands of biographies. The number of 'traits-units' collected exceeded 50,000. This impressive catalogue of traits was published by my laboratory in the form of bulky monographs.[7]

The material assembled allowed me to confirm my initial hypothesis. The planet/trait of character relationship is considerably more marked than the relationship between a planet and professional success.

GAUQUELIN 'PLUS ZONES' V. HOROSCOPE HOUSES

The connection between the horoscope and my observations is at the same time self-evident and contradictory. Although my conclusions may be superimposed on the horoscopic circle of houses they lead to a completely different interpretation.

According to these findings there are four zones of strong intensity, which I have named the 'plus zones'. Specialist circles have got into the habit of calling these regions of the sky the 'Gauquelin zones', which is quite flattering and, all things considered, a convenient way of defining them. So, there are four 'plus zones': when the planet has just risen, when it has reached its upper culmination (its 'noon'), when it has set and when it has passed its lower culmination (its 'midnight'). A person born when a planet occupies one of the four zones is likely to exhibit the psychological temperament associated with this planet.

However, two categories of 'plus zone' should be looked at more closely. The correlation between the planet and character is strongest when the planet has just risen, or when it has reached its upper culmination. The two other positions – when the planet is setting or when it is passing its lower culmination – are less powerful. When a planet is neither rising, nor at its culmination or setting, we say that it is in a zone of weak intensity, a 'minus zone'. When a planet occupies such a position at birth, there is little likelihood that the person will behave in a manner generally associated with

The Gauquelin Results

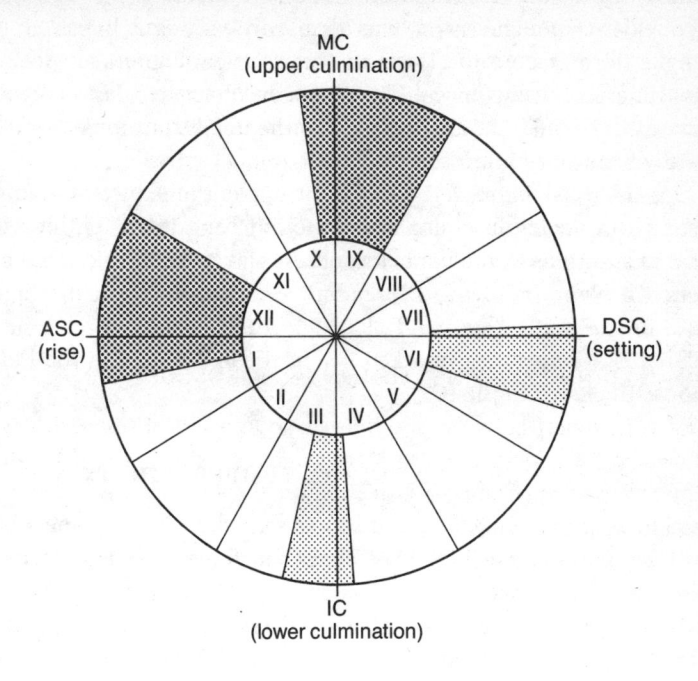

Figure 2: Gauquelin's 'plus zones' v. horoscope houses.

it. He or she is more likely to display the opposite characteristic tendencies.

But what do the terms 'rising', 'culmination' and 'setting' exactly mean when translated into astrological language? When we look at the representation of a horoscope we are immediately able to tell where the 'plus zones' are without concerning ourselves with astronomical information other than that required for the calculation of astrological houses.[8]

In Figure 2, the superimposition of 'plus zones' on the twelve astrological houses is illustrated. If the Moon, or one of the planets, is situated in one of the darkest sections in the figure, it is in one of the 'plus zones'. The rising 'plus zone' corresponds to house XII and to the third of house I closest to the Ascendant (marked 'ASC' on the diagram); the culmination 'plus zone' corresponds to house IX and to the third of house X closest to the middle of the sky (marked 'MC' in the figure).

On the other hand, if the Moon, or one of the planets, is situated in a lighter zone, it is also in a zone of strong intensity, although not as strong as in the darkest zone. As can be seen, this is the case when a planet is in the Descendant (marked 'DSC' in the figure) and in the half of house VI closest to the Descendant; or when a planet is at *imum coeli* (marked 'IC' in the figure) and in the half of house III closest to the IC.

THE FIVE PLANETARY TEMPERAMENTS

It is now time to indicate what sort of an influence the planets have on the personality when they appear in the above defined zones. Research on character traits has enabled me to describe five main types of personality: Jupiter, Saturn, Mars, Venus and the Moon. Despite our efforts, we have so far been unable to observe anything significant in connection with the Sun, Mercury and the planets beyond Saturn – Uranus, Neptune and Pluto. This presentation being only a brief summary of my work, I shall confine myself to supplying a list of twenty representative traits associated with the presence of Jupiter, Saturn, Mars, Venus or the Moon in the 'plus zones' (see Table 2). This a greatly abridged version of a list of traits which I have already published in works devoted to this question.[9]

THE HOROSCOPE AND THE 'GAUQUELIN EFFECT'

What is then left of the horoscope? As an illustration is worth more than a long discussion, it will suffice to compare the horoscope included in the previous chapter (see Figure 1, on p. 14) with Figure 3 below. The birth sky is the *same* but I have kept here only the

The Gauquelin Results

Table 2: Extract of twenty traits describing planetary types.

Jupiter	Saturn	Mars	Venus	Moon
ambitious	cold	active	affable	amiable
authoritarian	concentrated	ardent	agreeable	disorganized
conceited	conscientious	belligerent	ambiguous	dreamer
gay (merry)	discreet	brave	attractive	easy-going
harsh	introvert	combative	beloved	fashionable
humorous	methodical	daring	benevolent	friendly
independent	meticulous	dynamic	charming	generous
ironical	modest	energetic	considerate	good com-
lively	observant	fearless	courteous	pany
mocking	precise	fighter	elegant	good hearted
prodigal	reserved	lively	flattering	helpful
proud	sad	offensive	gallant	imaginative
show-off	simple	reckless	gracious	impressionable
social climber	sombre	spontaneous	juvenile	impulsive
spendthrift	stiff	strong-willed	kind	merry
talkative	taciturn	stormy	obliging	nonchalant
warm	thoughtful	tireless	pleasant	popular
well-off	timid	tough	poetic	socialite
witty	uncommunicative	valiant	polite	spontaneous
worldly	wise	vitality (full of)	seductive	superficial
				tolerant

astronomical factors whose influence has been empirically proved, namely five planets which occupy (or not) the 'plus zones' of the diurnal movement. That is all. In this case, only the planet Jupiter is in a 'plus zone'. The other planets are outside these zones. We can refer to Table 2 out of curiosity to check whether the traits listed under the Jupiter column are consistent overall with the character of the person. If this is the case, the 'Gauquelin effect' may be seen as a precious indicator.

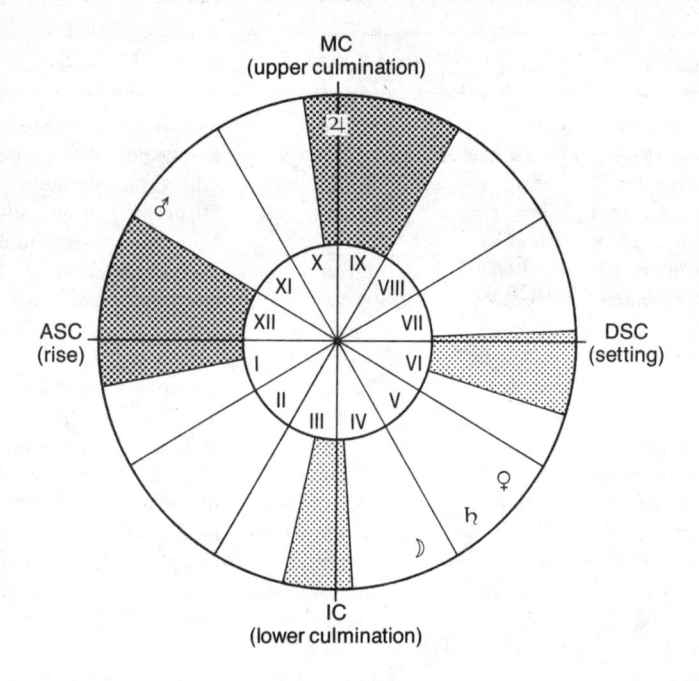

Figure 3: A neo-astrological interpretation:
Of all the elements of the horoscope presented in Figure 1 neo-astrology only considers five planets, whether or not they fall within the Gauquelin 'plus zones'.

It does provide, however, a striking contrast to all the interpretations that the astrologer claims to obtain from the classical birth sky as shown in Figure 1. Compared to the traditional horoscope, the 'Gauquelin horoscope', if I may say so, is only a skeleton, and an incomplete skeleton at that: the zodiac has disappeared, the aspects have disappeared, the houses have lost their significance. Out of the ten planets used by astrologers, only five are left. Can we still then call this astrology? This is to some extent a matter of opinion. There was a time when I claimed that the Gauquelin effect was not astrology at all, but, on reflection, the scientific adversaries who mockingly called me 'neo-astrologer' were not that wrong: I am, in fact, a neo-astrologer. The rest of this book will demonstrate this and the scientific community will judge whether there is any truth to the Gauquelin effect. I will show how science, despite its horror of astrological facts, has had to climb down before the evidence, and how some scientists have even cut off the branch of learning on which they thought themselves comfortably settled.

3

SCIENCE AND THE MARS EFFECT

In his work *The Copernican Revolution*, the science historian, Thomas Kuhn, wrote: 'A single observation incompatible with a theory demonstrates that the scientist has been employing the wrong theory all along. His conceptual scheme must then be abandoned and replaced.'[1] If he is correct, the problem of astrology's acceptability to science may be very easily resolved: it would be sufficient for astrology to produce 'a single observation incompatible' with the theory of the Universe which is the credo of modern science, and which excludes astrology. Were it not able to do this, astrology would remain confined to its intellectual ghetto.

Until my work, the scientific community had experienced no problem of conscience as far as astrology was concerned. The proof of astrological facts had not been produced. Of course, scientists despaired when they saw so many people reading horoscopes in the papers or going to consult an astrologer. They deplored the credulity of the clients and the greed of the casters of horoscopes. Nevertheless, their profound intellectual conviction was safe. At least it was until I came along with my 'magic potion', having spent my life verifying astrological assertions and disproving so many – particularly those concerning the signs of the zodiac – that I did not even appear to be an astrologer, but rather a critic. And yet here I was, claiming to have discovered that planets had an effect at birth and that statistical evidence proved it!

It is true that evidence of the effect of planets at birth may come as a shock to the scientist. 'If the Gauquelin planetary effects are real, they are truly astonishing and lie beyond anything that science can at present understand,' writes the UCLA astronomer George Abell.[2] The effects may be seen as all the more astonishing since the idea of planetary influences is nothing new. It is an ancient fancy in which people once believed, but which, it is thought, nothing could revive today. The 'grain of gold' in astrology appears to be as much of a utopia as the alchemist's gold. One may as well assert that the unicorn exists! Nevertheless, since I present facts, why not examine them?

This would be too simple. Science is no paradise. Thomas Kuhn observes in his classic work *The Structure of Scientific Revolutions*[3] that any science is, at a given moment in history, a prisoner of fundamental prejudices which he calls 'paradigms'. The paradigms are 'universally' accepted scientific truths which, for a time, provide the community of researchers with a model for all the problems and all their solutions.

History has shown that the shock produced by a new fact that is deemed incompatible with the paradigm of the epoch – what Kuhn calls the 'normal science' – is always severe. Hence the name 'revolution'. In their way, scientific revolutions, like social revolutions, are violent events: what they teach us at school, namely that scientists are prepared to accept factual evidence and, consequently, to revise their theory, is only a myth. On the contrary, they will fight tooth and nail against any element which may destroy it. What is more, they will use their paradigm as an argument to reject a priori what is threatening their intellectual cosiness. We know the pragmatic observation of Max Planck, the physics Nobel Prize winner:

> Great scientific theories do not usually conquer the world through being accepted by opponents who, gradually convinced of their truth, have finally adopted them. It is always very rare to find a Saul becoming a Paul. What happens is that the opponents of the new idea finally die off and the following generation grows up under its influence.[4]

Which is precisely how the Copernican revolution came to be. Paul Feyerabend, professor at the University of California at Berkeley, is a philosopher and the author of the much debated but very influential book, *Against Method*.[5] In this work he supports the thesis that science depends more on myth than on scientific philosophy. For him, science is nothing more than a way of thinking developed by man, but it is not necessarily the best way. And what is certain is that science is strident, tactless and arrogant.

Since prevention is better than cure, this 'strident and arrogant' science pronounced judgement upon astrology in 1975 behind closed doors. A group of 193 'leading scientists', among them nineteen Nobel Prize winners, signed a manifesto against astrology that appeared in the American magazine, *The Humanist*. This manifesto, published at the initiative of an eminent astronomer, Bart J. Bok, emeritus professor of astronomy at Harvard, was distributed to the media all over the world. The following sentence was pronounced without appeal:

> Those who wish to believe in astrology should realize that there is no scientific foundation for its tenets ... It is simply a mistake to imagine that the forces exerted by planets at the moment of birth can in any way shape our futures ... There is no verified scientific basis for astrology, and, indeed, there is strong evidence to the contrary.[6]

These three sentences, taken from the manifesto, set the tone. 'No verified scientific basis'? By 1975, I already had twenty years of publications behind me, as the astronomer Bok knew. But this he ignored as the following illustrates: 'It seems inconceivable that Mars and the Moon could produce mysterious waves, or vibrations that could affect our personalities in completely different ways.'[7] Precisely in the case of Mars, what could be more absurd, he maintained, that Gauquelin's claim that sports champions tend to be born when this planet rises or culminates?

Some scientists are so afraid of the paranormal that they have built fortresses to defend themselves against it and mustered troops to attack it. In 1949, the 'Comité pour l'Investigation scientifique des Phénomènes réputés paranormaux' (Committee for the Scientific Investigation of Paranormal Phenomena), also known in its abbreviated form 'Comité Para', was formed in Belgium. The United States waited until 1976 to create an anti-paranormal fighting machine,

Science and the Mars Effect

but theirs is now the most powerful one and the best organized, with contacts throughout the world. It is called the 'Committee for the Scientific Investigation of Claims of the Paranormal' (CSICOP) and its chairman is Paul Kurtz, professor of philosophy at the University of New York in Buffalo. (The French stronghold is called 'Comité français d'Études des Phénomènes paranormaux' (CFEPP).) The names are curiously similar and these organizations are fighting the same enemies. Among these, astrology is in the front line.

To avoid a sterile argument, I will now demonstrate how these committees function and why, so that they may be understood in the light of scientific revolutions.

First of all, they exist because science is going through a crisis. The paranormal is 'in the air', astrology is flourishing in people's minds. Did we not recently learn that the wife of a United States president used the services of an astrologer? What is worse, in the opinion of 'normal science', is that researchers of a scientific pedigree have set themselves the task of proving the existence of paranormal phenomena and claim to have succeeded. 'Normal science' has therefore had to mobilize against the potential invaders which may challenge the current theories and effect a formidable change in the scientific way of thinking. To the mind of such scientists, the integration of astrological facts to present knowledge would be an unthinkable revolution, and they are determined to defend themselves, particularly against the neo-astrology of Michel Gauquelin and his Mars effect. The following assertion is a measure of the impact of my work: 'Both those who are for and against astrology (in the broadest sense) as a serious field for study recognize the importance of Gauquelin's work. It is probably not putting it too strongly to say that everything (the evidence for any substantial kind of astrology) hangs on it.'[8] To destroy Gauquelin then would mean wiping out the most serious proof in favour of astrological reality. But what would happen if, by chance, this was not achieved?

The arguments of the various 'scientific committees' which have opposed me for thirty years are generally known under the name of

'The Mars Effect Controversy'. They have provoked many comments. If the files in my laboratory concerned with this polemic alone were placed one on top of another, they would form a pile ten feet high, and my documentation is still not complete. The history and details of these arguments have been told elsewhere.[9] In this work, I shall only present the main points in order to place it in the most general framework of the processes which normally precede a scientific revolution.

My observations were published for the first time in 1955.[10] In the same year, I contacted the Comité Para so that they could verify my work. The committee professed loud and clear that it was especially prepared for this task. In spite of this, however, I had to wait until 1968 for it to decide to repeat *one* of my experiments, that of the Mars effect on champions. For thirteen years I battled against a wall of silence, against a more or less disguised refusal to investigate, but the committee's decision (albeit belated) at least represented an admission that my work was of a scientific nature since it could be verified: it was, in the terminology of the scientific logician, Karl Popper, 'falsifiable', that is, it was possible to confirm or invalidate it through an experiment.[11]

The Comité Para collected the times of birth of 535 successful sportsmen, produced the calculations and discovered that it had repeated the Mars effect! Figure 4 allows us to see this at a glance. The frequency curve of Mars from the Comité Para group is so to speak superimposable upon mine. Yet, other sportsmen than mine were used in their experiment. The only thing left for the committee to do was to publish these results. But, for eight years they kept the Mars effect hidden away in their drawers, like a menacing reminder. It was not until 1976 that, under pressure, they produced a report.[12] What this long-deferred report did say, however, was that I had been mistaken in my methods and that the Mars effect was not proved. Why then wait so long to announce the good news to their colleagues? When I look at Figure 4, I think of Galileo's enemies who refused to look through his telescope and see Jupiter's satellites.

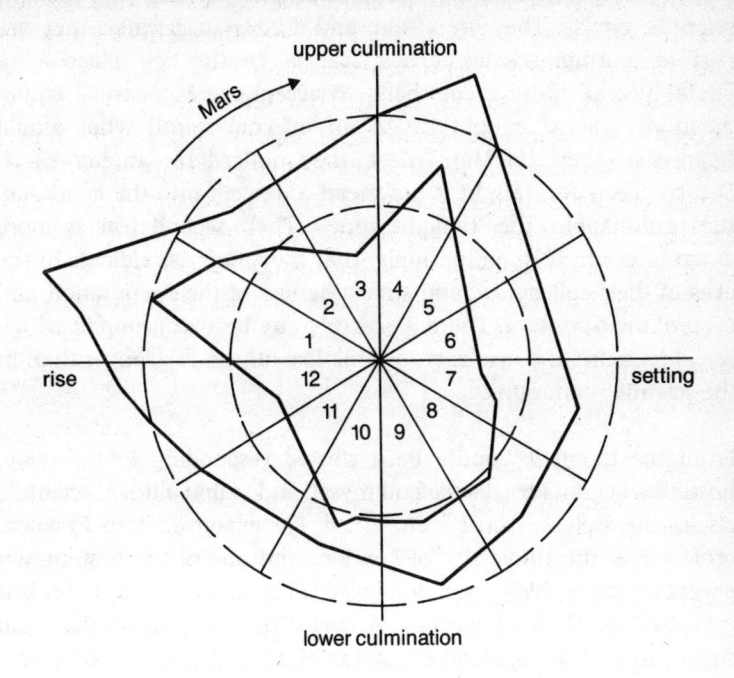

Figure 4: The Mars effect and sports champions:
A comparison between the occurrence of Mars in the twelve sectors as observed by Gauquelin (the outside curve represents the birth data on 1,553 sportsmen) and the one observed by the Belgian Comité Para (the inside curve represents the birth data on 535 other sportsmen). The two curves show that the greatest number of successful sportsmen is born after the rising or in the upper culmination of Mars (sectors 1 and 4). The two circles represent the possible occurrence at random frequency.

I am sure the members of the Comité Para are respectable citizens, but they are not honourable researchers: they have made a travesty of the truth and spread untruths about the Mars effect in scientific circles. They are afraid, and doubly so, because they are part of 'normal science'. Their fear is, in the first place, of a 'metaphysical' nature. For them, to accept the Mars effect would mean to become caught up in an infernal spiral: what would happen if, after the Mars effect, they noticed the Jupiter effect, Saturn effect, etc.? Might it not mean a descent into the irrational, the unthinkable, the 'twilight zone'? Their second fear is more down to earth. It is, quite simply, that they may risk ridicule in the eyes of their colleagues, and suffer the loss of their reputation and even of their position. There is scarcely any human group in which social pressure, the necessity to think like others, is stronger than in the scientific community.

From the moment Comité Para started responding in this way, hostilities began. I tried to defend myself and to find allies in scientific circles themselves. And I found them. For example, Hans Eysenck, professor of the University of London, and one of the best-known psychologists of his generation, pleaded in my favour: 'I think it may be said that, as far as objectivity of observation, statistical significance of differences, verification of the hypothesis, and replicability are concerned, there are few sets of data which in psychology could compete with these observations.'[13] There were researchers who did agree to look into Galileo's telescope, but the committee also found its allies, mostly among astronomers. And this conflict, that had at first been limited to two protagonists, the committee and myself, spread and eventually reached the United States, where the famous anti-astrological manifesto had just been published, accompanied by an article by Lawrence Jerome, describing my work as a perfect example of statistical error. I leapt at the opportunity this offered me and demanded, and was granted, right of reply. I then was able to demonstrate that Jerome was an ignoramus and I mentioned my success against the Comité Para. As a result, the committee was contacted by Paul Kurtz, editor of *The Humanist* at the time. The scientists defended themselves in a curious fashion, acknowledging that they had indeed replicated the 'Mars effect' but concluding that it was meaningless. They asserted that my method contained an error but were unable to point it out (and for a very good reason: they could not find it).

Kurtz, who had received numerous letters of protest about Jerome's criticism of me, nevertheless remained convinced that I was wrong and, in order to prove this to his readers, consulted Marvin Zelen, professor of biostatistics at Harvard. Zelen proposed a control test, which everyone – especially the members of the newly formed American committee (CSICOP) – judged would be 'crucial'. I thus proceeded to carry out the 'Zelen Test' under the watchful eyes of Kurtz, Zelen and Abell, the UCLA astronomer, who had joined them. To the confusion of the American committee the control test clearly went my way. The results were published in *The Humanist* in 1977.[14]

Desolation reigned in the CSICOP camp. In an attempt to save face, Kurtz, Zelen and Abell published an article in which they tried to deny the significance of the control test and questioned my intellectual integrity.[15] They were often to be reproached for this article, not only by observers who were outsiders to the polemic, but also by certain members of the CSICOP itself, who resigned in protest. One astronomer, Dennis Rawlins, created a great stir in doing so and published a formidable document, *sTarbaby*, directed against his old colleagues. Having been a privileged witness in the wings of the polemic, he vigorously denounced the somewhat confused and even irrational behaviour of some CSICOP members in this affair.[16] The argument flared up and Rawlins's article reached the media. Each party, in turn, vehemently intervened.

In the early 1980s, the dispute over the Mars effect was to become a *model* for historians of science studying the irrational reaction of the scientific community when confronted with a 'paranormal' phenomenon it could not destroy. Trevor Pinch and H. Collins,[17] Marcello Truzzi,[18] Henry Krips[19] and some others engaged in analyses of the Mars effect. Henceforth it became a classic.

In 1983, the polemic at last died down after the publication in *The Skeptical Inquirer*, the CSICOP official journal, of an article signed by Abell, Kurtz and Zelen. After pressure from critics, the trio found it preferable to admit to their errors. They confessed that they had not always been 'careful' in their judgements, and even went as far as publicly disclaiming their colleagues in Comité Para. 'Gauquelin adequately allowed for demographic and astronomical factors in predicting the expected distribution of Mars sectors for birth times in the general population.'[20] The dispute, which had gone on for thirty years, ended in my favour. The accuracy of my methods and results was at last acknowledged. (Could this be the beginning of official recognition of neo-astrology?)

Subsequently, in 1988, came the publication of the important work of Dr Suitbert Ertel, professor of psychology at the University of Göttingen, in what was West Germany before the reunification, dealing with the relationship between celebrity and the intensity of the Mars effect. Turning again to the data that has been gathered on 4,000 sportsmen, Ertel demonstrated through a rigorous analysis that the Mars effect operates to a striking degree: the more famous the champions, the more pronounced the Mars effect at birth. 'Such a result,' concludes Ertel, 'cannot be explained away by an error of method or a manipulation of birth data by Gauquelin.'[21]

The Mars effect has in this way been proved 'beyond any reasonable doubt', and although this represents only a *single* observation among the dozens that I have published, if we recall what Thomas Kuhn writes on the subject of scientific revolutions: 'A *single* observation incompatible with a theory demonstrates that the scientist has been employing the wrong theory all along. His conceptual scheme . . . must then be abandoned and replaced.'[22]

Even on its own, the Mars effect obliges scientists to revise their theory of the Universe. Coming at the end of the twentieth century, this may be a very bitter pill for them to swallow. How can the Universe contain at the same time galaxies, quasars, black holes as well as the influence of Mars at the birth of a future champion? Is it necessary to reinstate the astrological facts long since rejected as merely superstition? Could it be that they have not been *only* superstition after all, but rather, lost knowledge, a lost idea? This is in fact what happened in the field of astronomy with the ideas of Aristarchos of Samos.

First Interlude:

IN SEARCH OF A LOST PARADIGM

As we all know, Copernicus (1473–1543), transformed our vision of the world when, in 1543, he decided to place the Sun in the centre of the Universe and have the Earth revolve around it. From the time of Ptolemy, the great astronomer of antiquity who lived in the second century A.D., man had believed the world to be geocentric: the Earth in the centre and the Sun circling around it.

'Few scientific theories have played so large a role in non-scientific thought,' writes Thomas Kuhn in his book, *The Copernican Revolution*.[1] Because Copernicus reduced the Earth to the status of a simple planet, man was no longer the centre of the universe. Together with the science of astronomy, philosophy and religion were critically re-examined. This is why, before it became established, the Copernican theory met with such strong opposition, above all from the Church, since it ran contrary to the Scriptures.

Yet, as the science historian, George Sarton, mentions it is a very old idea. A Greek astronomer, Aristarchos of Samos, who lived in the third century B.C., 'had conceived what we call the Copernican universe, eighteen centuries before Copernicus. The name that has been given to him in modern times, "The Copernicus of Antiquity", is fully deserved.'[2]

The treatise in which Aristarchos laid out his hypothesis has been lost; however, Sarton continues:

> We know it only through his younger contemporary Archimedes. It is best to quote Archimedes's own words in his *Sand Reckoner*; a sensitive person cannot read them without emotion when he remembers that they were written before 216 B.C.:

Neo-Astrology

'You are aware that universe (cosmos) is the name given by most astronomers to the sphere whose centre is the centre of the Earth, and whose radius is equal to the distance between the centre of the Sun and the centre of the Earth. This is the common account as you have heard from astronomers. But Aristarchos of Samos brought out a book consisting of some hypotheses, wherein it appears, as a consequence of assumptions made, that the real universe is many times greater than the one just mentioned. His hypotheses are that the fixed stars and the Sun remain unmoved, that the Earth revolves about the Sun in the circumference of a circle, the Sun lying in the middle orbit, and that the sphere of the fixed stars, situated about the same centre as the Sun, is so great that the circle in which he supposes the Earth to revolve bears such a proportion to the distance of the fixed stars as the centre of the sphere bears to its surface.'

To put it in plainer words, Aristarchos of Samos had put the centre of the universe in the Sun (instead of the Earth) and assumed the daily rotation of the Earth around its own axis and the yearly rotation of the Earth around the Sun. All the planets circle around the Sun except the Moon, which alone circles around the Earth ... This is stupendous, and would be incredible, if we had it from another source, but we have no reason to doubt Archimedes, who was born within Aristarchos's lifetime and might have known him personally. Moreover, why should he invent such a statement? Had he invented it, it would be just as stupendous.[3]

Unfortunately, this hypothesis was then rejected by Hipparchus, and since he was regarded as the greatest astronomer of antiquity, the principle of authority played against Aristarchos. Two centuries later, when Ptolemy wrote his famous astronomical treatise, *Almagest*, he forgot Aristarchos's idea. *Almagest* was to remain *the* reference book for all the astronomers until Copernicus. It is true that Ptolemy was a great astronomer and achieved a high degree of precision in predicting the position of planets, thanks to a complex system of epicycles (compounded circular orbits). But even an ever more complicated system of epicycles was not enough to completely reconcile theory and observation. The real solution was found in the Copernican revolution which stipulated that the Earth and the planets revolve around the Sun, and that there are no epicycles. However, according to Thomas Kuhn, the revolution was an incredibly long time coming:

First Interlude: In Search of a Lost Paradigm

> For almost 1800 years, from the time of Hipparchus until the birth of Copernicus, the conception of compounded circular orbits within an earth-centred universe dominated every technically developed attack upon the problem of the planets, and there were a great many such attacks before Copernicus. Despite its slight but recognized inaccuracy and its striking lack of economy, the developed Ptolemaic system had an immense life span, and the longevity of this magnificent but clearly imperfect system poses ... puzzles ... how was the psychological grip of this traditional approach to a traditional problem released? Or to put the same question more directly: Why was the Copernican revolution so delayed?[4]

Kuhn proposes discerning answers to this question, but to discuss this would lead me too far astray, too far from astrology.

Let us remember this lesson. Astronomy made no conclusive progress for 1,800 years. Even so, it is a science. My question is this: Why was the the 'Copernican revolution' of *astrology* so delayed? To pose this question is not as strange as it may seem at first. Since the beginning of civilization, astronomy and astrology have been sister doctrines – twin sisters, who had come out of the same mould, and sprung from the same idea. In antiquity, astronomy was not thought of as a science, or astrology as a pseudo-science. This idea spread much later.

Ptolemy thus regarded astronomy and astrology as two equally respectable doctrines. In his mind, the one did not go without the other. He was also to write *Tetrabiblos*, an astrological treatise. Few works have had such a profound and lasting influence as this treatise. Some 1,800 years later, contemporary astrology is none other than Ptolemy's astrology slightly adapted to modern vocabulary. 1,800 years. This is precisely the span of time that separated Aristarchos from Copernicus. The parallel between astrology and astronomy is striking.

'Why Astrology is a Pseudo-Science' is the title of the thesis recently defended by a science philosopher, Paul Thagard. He explains: 'To get a criterion demarcating astrology from science, we need to consider it in a wider historical and social context.' He then proposes the following principles of demarcation:

Neo-Astrology

> A theory or discipline which purports to be scientific is *pseudo-scientific* if and only if: (1) it has been less progressive than alternative theories over a long period of time, and faces many unsolved problems; and (2) the community of practitioners makes little attempt to develop the theory towards solutions of the problems, shows no concern for attempts to evaluate the theory in relation to others, and is selective in considering confirmations and disconfirmations ... This principle captures, I believe, what is most importantly unscientific about astrology. First, astrology is dramatically unprogressive, in that it has changed little and has added nothing to its explanatory power since the time of Ptolemy ... and finally, the community of astrologers is generally unconcerned with advancing astrology to deal with outstanding problems or with evaluating the theory in relation to others. For these reasons, my criterion marks astrology as pseudoscientific.[5]

Thagard's analysis is interesting. It is true that, until now, astrology has been 'dramatically unprogressive' and that astrologers have had little inclination to resolve the obvious incompatibilities through modern science. But, had he lived a little while before Copernicus, he may well have applied his criteria to *astronomy* and called it a pseudo-scientific doctrine. Astronomy was *also* 'dramatically unprogressive' between the times of Ptolemy and Copernicus, and the astronomers of this long period were 'generally unconcerned' with the 'outstanding problems' generated by, for example, the theory of epicycles. Of course, since its Copernican revolution, astronomy has had Kepler, Newton and Einstein.

However, astrology, in its turn, has just entered a full-blown revolution, four centuries after astronomy, which is a very short period in historical terms. The dictatorship of the Greek horoscope has fallen under the democratic blow of statistics. From chaos, a revolutionary doctrine is emerging, that of *neo-astrology*. It should not be ungrateful towards traditional astrology since it was created from it: I did not discover the Mars effect *ex nihilo*, but because astrological literature already existed, and this is true of all my observations. I would like to set out a daring theory: during its long history, astrology has known many an 'Aristarchos of Samos'. Whether anonymous authors or famous people, they have been the

First Interlude: In Search of a Lost Paradigm

inventors or guardians of a treasure hidden among the horoscopic 'epicycles'. Without always being conscious of it, they have preserved the essence for us, through the centuries, civilizations, wars and religions.

True astrology – that of the Mars effect – is a lost paradigm, and although this is still only a hypothesis, the answer perhaps lies in the analysis of documents from the past.

ACT TWO

The Babylonians

4

ON THE WAY TO THE HOROSCOPE

Is it reasonable to go back to the Babylonians to find the predecessors of the Gauquelin effects? Archaeologists describe Babylonian astrology with a certain contempt while professing evident respect for Babylonian astronomy, which was based on 'an admirable mathematical theory', 'although the Babylonians themselves gave astrology a pre-eminent place. It is my opinion, however, that these scholars are prisoners of the scientific paradigm which holds sway today and according to which they judge the Babylonians. I believe that since neo-astrology is scientifically proved, it is perfectly legitimate to return to the Babylonians. After all, they were the inventors of the astrological paradigm, the first to develop the basic postulate that the planets have an influence at birth.

Of course, we must resist the temptation of attributing to the Babylonians discoveries which they did not actually make. But we must also seek every particle of astrological truth in the statements of these people, at once so close to us and so distant in time and manner of thinking. For the Babylonians, astronomy and astrology always went together, the first being necessary to the second. Progress in astronomy went hand in hand with the advances in astrology. How much the Babylonians deserve the title of predecessors of a kind of neo-astrology can be seen through a careful analysis of the published works and commentaries of the greatest experts – Neugebauer, Van der Waerden, and Sachs.

Who were, in fact, the Babylonians? This general term refers, according to the specialists, to a civilization stretching across more than a thousand years. We distinguish between the Old Babylonians, who lived between 1300 and 800 B.C., and the New Babylonians, who existed from around 700 to 300 B.C. In addition, 'Babylonian' is a generic term referring to the peoples who lived in the various cities of Mesopotamia. The Babylonians did not all live in Babylon itself, but in Ur, Uruk, Nineveh, etc., all of which contributed, sometimes even more than Babylon, to the development of astronomy and astrology. But Babylon's fame, the splendour of its hanging gardens, its famous ziggurat – the biblical Tower of Babel – made its name the symbol of a whole civilization.

Our knowledge of Babylonian culture comes from the cuneiform writings on clay tablets that were found by chance in excavations and deciphered. These are 'first-hand' documents, unaltered over the centuries by careless copiers or by historians with too much imagination, and they constitute the legacy of a civilization particularly prolific in wars, massacres and destruction. In his book, *The Exact Sciences in Antiquity*, Otto Neugebauer, one of the greatest scholars on this subject, notes: 'Without violent catastrophes there would hardly be any archaeology. If Mesopotamian cities had not been turned into desert hills, we would have no chance of finding the hundreds of thousands of documents from which Babylonian history is written.'[2]

Nonetheless, what we do know remains very fragmented. Not only because most of the finds were largely a matter of chance but mostly, and paradoxically, because *too many* cuneiform tablets have come to light. The experts have not had enough time to translate them and the backlog is accumulating at the speed of Third World debts.

To quote Neugebauer again: 'It is barely a hundred years since cuneiform writing once more became intelligible ... But while decipherment and interpretation progressed in slow steps, texts were found in tremendous number from the very beginning.'[3] Those in the ruins of Khorsabad, near Mosul, were the first to be discovered, in 1848, then came the Nineveh library in 1850, followed by the Ashurbanipal library in 1853. In total, some 20,000 tablets are in storage at the British Museum. Neugebauer continues:

On the Way to the Horoscope

> Perhaps about a quarter of these collections is published today ... This ratio between existing and published texts might seem rather small. Actually it is unusually high and only due to the fact that it is the result of a century of work on one of the most famous discoveries in the Near East. In the meantime, many tens of thousands of tablets have found their way into museums, providing source material which would require several centuries for their publication even under the concentrated efforts of all living Assyriologists.[4]

This is quite depressing. Anyone for Assyriology?

The tablets which will lie untranslated for another couple of centuries in the cellars of the British Museum or elsewhere may hold the most important secrets on Babylonian astrology. But what has been published so far is already worth the effort.

In the first chapter, I spoke of the Sumerians, the people who preceded the Babylonians in Mesopotamia. They recognized gods in the astral trio of Sun-Moon-Venus, and addressed prayers to them. This rather primitive astral religion surely arose out of adoration rather than prediction. The Old Babylonians went further. It was not enough for them to adore the gods, they had to predict their feelings. As for the New Babylonians, they went even further still. It was between the two that the transition from astral religion to real astrology was effected.

The Old Babylonians at first enriched and refined the Sumerian tradition. They knew all the planets of the solar system which are visible to the eye: Mercury, Venus, Mars, Jupiter, Saturn. From the beginning – and this very beginning is unfortunately still a mystery – the symbol of each star was clearly defined. In his book *Science Awakening*, Van der Waerden writes:

> As far as we know, the Babylonians always identified the planets with gods or at least allocated them to their gods. Jupiter was Marduk, i.e. 'star god Marduk', or 'star of the god Marduk'. Venus was identified with Ishtar, the goddess of love, Mars with the wargod Nergal. Correspondingly, the astrological interpretations of Mars phenomena relate mostly to war and destruction. The Venus omina deal frequently with love and fertility.[5]

Neo-Astrology

The series of tablets called 'Enuma Anu Enlil' marked the beginning of a primitive code of prediction: 'When Mars approaches the star SHU.GI, there will be uprising in Amurru and hostility; one will kill another ... When Venus stands high, pleasure of copulation ... When Venus stands in her place, ... "fullness" of the women shall there be in the land ...'[6] These texts date from 1400 B.C. and only correspond, in Van der Waerden's words, to the 'prehistory of Babylonian astronomy'. Mars is *already* linked to war and aggression; Venus is *already* linked to pleasure and love. Thirty-three centuries later the same opposition between Mars and Venus can be found in my work. But this is not the place to be reaching conclusions.

In a slightly grumpy scholarly manner, Neugebauer does not allow us to cherish any illusion. He states that the proverbial brilliance of the Babylonian sky is more a literary cliché than a real fact. The closeness of the desert, with its sandstorms, often obscured the horizon. 'This is even more regrettable,' he says, 'since the majority of problems in which the Babylonian astronomers were interested are phenomena close to the horizon.'[7] Van der Waerden corroborates this: 'The observation of the rising and setting of stars near the horizon is very easily disturbed by the varying conditions of the atmosphere.'[8]

Why – if not for astrological reasons – would the Babylonians attach so much importance to the rising and setting of the stars when the conditions were so unfavourable? In any case, they persisted and overcame the difficulty with remarkable ingenuity. If a star was lost in the mist on the horizon, they were still able to determine its rising, thanks to the observation of a *ziqpu*-star.

A *ziqpu*-star is a star which reaches its upper culmination in the middle of the sky. A text from the mulAPIN series of cuneiform tablets says: 'The *ziqpu*-stars (are those) which stand in the path of Enlil in the middle of the sky across from the chest of the observer of the sky, and by means of which the rising and setting of the stars are observed by night.' A list of *ziqpu*-stars and of examples of procedures is then included, of which the following item is an example: 'To observe the *ziqpu*, set yourself on the morning of 20

On the Way to the Horoscope

Nisannu before sunrise, the West to your right, the East to your left, your eyes to the South: then *kumara sha* (the name of a star) ... is to be found in the middle of the sky across from your chest and mul GAM (another star) is rising.' With the ingenuity of the expert who thinks all must be evident to everyone Van der Waerden writes:

> This description makes it clear beyond any possible doubt that *ziqpu* is the Babylonian technical term for culmination ... When, therefore, bad atmospheric conditions prevented the direct observation of the rising of GAM, it was possible to observe instead the simultaneous culmination of *kumara sha* which means 'shoulder of the griffin'; and so on.[9]

The series of *astronomical* tablets, mulAPIN, dates from the end of Assyrian rule (1000–612 B.C.). It has its *astrological* counterpart in the series of tablets, *Enuma Anu Enlil.* They are the omens written by the astrologers of Assyrian kings. In this period, the Babylonians succeeded in calculating the rising, setting and culmination of the stars in order to obtain astrological omens. This is still far from the Gauquelin 'plus zones', because it is a matter here of stars, not of planets; the culmination in itself is not considered a bearer of the omen; birth is not mentioned. In fact, Van der Waerden asserts categorically: 'Omen Astrology is not concerned with birth horoscopes and it does not use zodiacal signs. For the application to Omen Astrology the astronomy of mulAPIN is perfectly sufficient.'[10]

However, the Babylonians of the Assyrian period were, despite everything, on the right path: ready to reach a major stage in their knowledge of astronomy. This progress was to lead them to a new type of astrology, zodiacal astrology. This was probably their goal.

The zodiacal circle was known to the Babylonians before 700 B.C.; the mulAPIN text lists some fifteen constellations and writes that the Sun, Moon and planets follow this path. This is still vague. It is not until the cuneiform writings dated 419 B.C., that for the first time a new system appears. Then, the position of a planet is noted by indicating in which sign it appears. The text contains observations similar to the following: 'Jupiter and Venus at the beginning of Cancer, Mars in Leo, Saturn in Pisces. Twenty-ninth day: Mercury's evening setting in Taurus.'[11] In the time of the Seleucids (312–64 B.C.) the tables for the Moon and the planets were even more sophisticated: the positions were calculated mathematically and marked in zodiacal signs and degrees. The signs are all exactly the same length: 30 degrees each.

A text from the end of the Babylonian epoch, published by a French Assyriologist, Thureau-Dangin, and taken from tablets discovered in Uruk, lists the famous twelve constellations or signs of the zodiac: 'Aries, Pleiades (Taurus), Gemini, Praesepe (Cancer), Leo, Spica (Virgo), Libra, Scorpio, Sagittarius, Capricorn, Aquarius, Pisces.' This remarkable achievement had an astrological goal. Van der Waerden remarks:

> We know from cuneiform texts that stars were worshipped as Gods. For the zodiacal signs or constellations we have three magical texts, published by Ungnad, prescribing to repeat the names of the signs a certain number of times in different cases. This proves that the zodiacal signs were considered as mighty powers.[12]

In this way, the Babylonians passed from Omen Astrology to Zodiacal Astrology. For the latter, the use of the twelve signs of the zodiac is obviously essential, 'but it has nothing to do with birth horoscopes'.[13] At least for the time being. The discovery of the zodiac was not only a remarkable astronomical advance. Zodiacal Astrology is the *necessary transition* leading the Babylonians to their third type of astrology, the one we know today: Horoscopic Astrology. Their final stage.

5

AN EARLY 'GRAIN OF GOLD'?

I first met Jean Hiéroz (1889–1981) in 1955. Hiéroz, whose real name was Jean Rosière, was a former student of École Navale and a prosperous businessman. He is known as an astrologer but he was, above all, passionate about the history of astrology. He also had, incidentally, a sharp tongue. In *Les Cahiers Astrologiques* (a well-known French astrological journal), to which he contributed regularly, he often put in their place those astrologers who were ignorant about probability calculus and the history of astrology.

Shortly after *L'influence des astres*[1] came out, Hiéroz invited me to his Paris apartment on the Champs Élysées for a drink and to discuss my work. He was curious to meet the young man of twenty-six (he was sixty-six at the time) who had presumed to 'clean up' the astrological scene at one statistical stroke by publishing the birth data of 6,000 famous people. He showed me his astrological library, of which he was very proud and rightly so as it was unique. I remember how amazed I was at the sight of originals by ancient authors, mostly written in Latin, which he read fluently.

However, this love of the past did not prevent Hiéroz from keeping in touch with the latest specialized publications on the history of astrology. He also read English with facility and had just received a scholarly article, by A. Sachs, of Brown University, entitled simply 'Babylonian Horoscopes'.[2] He recommended that I read it and very obligingly passed on to me a copy.

My English was not great in those days and my mind was more concerned with compiling statistics than with deciphering the astrological past. Nevertheless, the article left quite an impression on me, and I mentioned it subsequently on several occasions in my works, especially in *The Cosmic Clocks*, which appeared in 1967.

I have always admired the knowledge of this author, who introduces us, through his erudition, to a completely new world of ideas. Today, however, I no longer believe that these ideas are as strange as they seem and consider that a *re-reading* of Sachs's fundamental article should be undertaken in the light of its astrological content.

I should now like to analyse Sachs's article in a 'disrespectful' manner, that is to say to extract from it, if possible, all the notions of Babylonian horoscopes which, in one way or another, could possibly have anticipated the Gauquelin effects. Although Sachs may be shocked at this he need not worry: I shall be as respectful of his text as I am disrespectful in my intentions! Not to play the game would be dishonest, and more seriously, it would be wasting time. The subject is too serious for that.

The essence of what we know today about Babylonian horoscopes is contained in Sachs's article. Though it is not very recent (1952), it has not been invalidated by subsequent publications. On the contrary, it still remains the standard work on the subject.

First of all, Sachs recognizes the Babylonians' undoubted historical precedence over the Greeks in the development of horoscopic astrology:

> The basic idea of horoscopic astrology was first propounded in Babylonia. Quite aside from the fact that horoscopes were actually cast there before Hellenistic times, it can scarcely be doubted that three of the necessary elements were to be found *par excellence* in Babylonia of, say, the last two centuries of the Persian period (400–300 B.C.): the belief that celestial events can be used systematically to predict the future, the belief that predictions can be made for an individual's future, and the existence of the zodiac.[3]

I would like to add a rider to the second element, namely: 'the belief that predictions can be made for an individual'. Horoscopic astrology – the horoscope – rests on the *extremely bold* hypothesis that the sky at birth has an influence on the fate of the newborn.

We are not always aware of the intellectual revolution that took

An Early 'Grain of Gold'?

place in this period among the Babylonians. Before the creation of the horoscope, the stars served to predict events, wars, sandstorms, plagues of locusts. Man, as an individual, was not involved. Then, all at once – no one knows how – a completely different idea emerged. To use the current buzzword, there was a fundamental paradigm shift. This was the most important turning point in the history of astrology, which still today in essence depends on the sky at birth for its existence. Whether the Babylonian hypothesis was a stroke of genius or nonsensical is a different matter, although if the Gauquelin effects continue to be recognized by science, it could be said that it was, *fundamentally*, a hypothesis born of genius, whoever's idea it was. Sachs can only state:

> Once the zodiac was invented, the biggest and most difficult step then had to be taken: the systematization of the 'qualities' of the planets and the signs of the zodiac combined with some operational procedure leading to predictions on the basis of specific positions. In the present state of our knowledge, this is *the most obscure step of all.*[4] [My emphasis.]

Neugebauer confirms this: 'It should be admitted that we know next to nothing about the details of horoscopic astrology in Mesopotamia, in sharpest contrast to the overwhelming abundance of astrological documents from Hellenistic Egypt and the Roman and Byzantine period.'[5] Indeed, there is no known document in existence at this time which throws any real light on the turning point in thinking that is the astrological hypothesis *par excellence*, according to which man's soul is, at birth, marked by the indelible stamp of the celestial spheres. The answer *may* lie in the clay tablets which will be translated by Assyriologists in the future. The discovery of this 'missing link' in the history of ideas *could be* the key to many of the problems science has had to contend with as a result of the Gauquelin effect.

Fortunately, we are a lot better informed about the horoscopes themselves than about their origin. According to Sachs the first known horoscope dates from 410 B.C.: 'If I am right – and I do not see wherein I might have erred – in restoring the date of the earliest

Neo-Astrology

cuneiform horoscope as 410 B.C.'[6] The Babylonian horoscopes collected by him, which date from 410 to 141 B.C., are an amazing source of documentation. Nevertheless, they leave the astrologer of today hungry for more. These horoscopes are astronomically elementary, and their interpretations, when they are not illegible, are even more so. 'We do not yet have a single text of a general character which correlates the planets' being in the various zodiacal signs with personal predictions,'[7] Sachs remarks. In other words, there are still no 'text-books'. We will need to wait for the Greeks to find them.

Here is an example of Babylonian horoscope, chosen in preference to some others because the interpretations have been relatively well preserved. The birth took place in the morning of 3 June 235 B.C. The translation of the cuneiform writings reads as follows:

> Year 77 of the Seleucid era, month Simab, from the fourth day, in the last part of the night of the fifth day, Aristokrates was born.
> The day: Moon in Leo. Sun is 12:30° in Gemini.
> The Moon sets its face from the middle toward the top; (the relevant omen reads:) If from the middle toward the top, it (i.e. the Moon) sets its face (there will ensue) destruction.
> Jupiter . . . in 18° Sagittarius. The place of Jupiter (means):
> His life (will be) regular, well; he will become rich, he will grow old (his) days will be numerous (literally, long).
> Venus in 4° Taurus. The place of Venus (means):
> Wherever he may go, it will be favourable (for him): he will have sons and daughters.
> Mercury in Gemini, with the Sun. The place of Mercury (means):
> The brave one will be first in rank, he will be more important than his brothers.
> Saturn: 6° Cancer. Mars 24° Cancer . . . (the end of the prediction was destroyed).

'It is interesting to note,' comments Sachs, 'that here we have a horoscope cast for a man bearing a Greek name and born in the early part of the Seleucid period. It is not difficult (though perhaps not correct) to picture him, a member of the second or third generation of the ruling classes, sufficiently curious or superstitious to have his fortune told by a proud but willing native priest at Uruk.'[8]

An Early 'Grain of Gold'?

These horoscopes lack basic astrological facts, such as the Ascendant and so cannot be called true horoscopes. To quote Sachs again: 'No Babylonian horoscope mentions the Horoscopus (the computed zodiacal sign or point rising at the time of birth) or any of the other secondary astrological positions which play important roles in Greco-Roman astrology.'[9]

No 'Horoscopus' – today this is called the Ascendant, which makes the terminology less confusing – means that there was no division at this stage of the diurnal movement into astrological houses. It was only later that the Greeks made these essential contributions. There is no trace of the Gauquelin effect in these Babylonian horoscopes (the Gauquelin zones – see Figure 2, on p. 27 – require the rising and culmination of the planets to be taken into consideration). At this point, the neo-astrologer in search of his origins cannot help but feel a degree of disappointment.

However, Sachs includes in his article the translation of *other tablets*. Before him, in 1922, Thureau-Dangin had already made a partial translation of tablets called 'Uruk Tablets' because they were found under the ruins of that city. Often mentioned by specialists in this field, these refer to individual predictions, though according to Sachs: 'strictly speaking, these omens should not be called horoscopic since the signs of the zodiac are nowhere mentioned; in fact, all the phenomena can occur anywhere in the zodiac. These pseudo-horoscopic omens may reflect a pre-horoscopic level of development.'[10]

I have read and re-read Thureau-Dangin and Sachs many times, and have noted that their translations are very close, which is, it must be said, very reassuring for the science of Assyriology. I have always been intrigued, even excited, by what I read because these omens refer to the rising and setting of the Moon and planets, an area of astronomy which is dear to me.

Let us read together the omens 27–33. They are worth it:

27 If a child is born when the Moon has come forth (then his life will be) bright, excellent, regular, and long.
28 If a child is born when the Sun has come forth (then) . . . (the interpretation is missing).

29 If a child is born when Jupiter has come forth, (then his life will be) regular, well; he will become rich, he will grow old, (his) days will be long.
30 If a child is born when Venus has come forth, (then his life will be) exceptionally calm; wherever he may go, it will be favourable; his days will be long.
31 If a child is born when Mercury has come forth, (then his life will be) brave, lordly; ...
32 If a child is born when Mars has come forth, then ..., hot(?) temper(?).
33 If a child is born when Saturn has come forth, (then his life will be) dark, obscure, sick, and constrained.

If one favours the theory that the Babylonians are the true precursors of neo-astrology – anonymous 'Aristarchoses of Samos' – then these texts offer a real occasion for enthusiasm.

First of all, the term 'has come forth' means 'which has just risen'. All the cuneiform scholars agree on this. The texts are then in fact saying: 'If a child is born when the Moon is rising ...' (etc.). There is no doubt that here the Babylonians are in the process of interpreting the position of the Moon and of the planets when they are found in the Gauquelin zone of rising. Moreover, the influence attributed to each rising planet is strangely similar to the key-words describing planetary types, which I and my team painstakingly brought to light by assembling 50,000 traits of character (see Table 2, on p. 29).

Of course, the omens are too short and clumsily worded. Furthermore, my reading is somewhat selective. In our work, the Moon is not particularly linked to the words 'bright', 'excellent', 'regular'; nor is Mercury to the epithets 'brave' and 'lordly'. But it may be that the Babylonians are right after all.

Furthermore, *rightly or wrongly*, these few scraps of interpretation habour the seed of what was to become the planetary symbolism of all astrological periods. Let us refer to the section entitled 'The Role of the Planets' in the chapter 'The Horoscope in a Nutshell'. The predictions for Venus and Jupiter are the most favourable: for Venus, 'exceptionally calm', and for Jupiter, 'well' and 'rich'. In fact, present-day astrology places Venus and Jupiter among the

An Early 'Grain of Gold'?

'beneficent' planets, whereas the predictions for Mars and Saturn are less favourable: the terms used for Mars are 'aggression', 'hot temper', and for Saturn, 'misfortunes'. This is why contemporary astrology places Mars and Saturn among the 'malefic' planets. Already there are contours of expansive Jupiter versus 'constrained' Saturn, and of 'calm' Venus against 'violent' Mars, two antagonistic pairs that still find relevance today, beyond the field of astrology. In medicine, the male child is represented by the ideogram of Mars (♂) and the female, by the ideogram of Venus (♀), implying that boys are more boisterous than girls.

The perennial quality of much of the role played by the planet-gods after twenty-five centuries is already rather surprising. What can we then say about the (probable) fact that this role was recently confirmed by statistical inquiry? What did the Babylonians do to arrive at this point? They did not after all have innate knowledge of these things. It is a little disappointing to see them go astray in casting omens from the position of *fixed stars* at birth. To quote from the tablet translation again: 'When Herculis comes forth, he will be poor ... When Andromedae comes forth, death [caused] by a snake [etc.]' The inclusion of the fixed stars into the planetary concert is slightly discordant to us. Not so to the Babylonians.

The following extracts taken from tablets refer to the setting of planets. For example: 'If a child is born when Venus has set, then ...' Unfortunately, the interpretation was destroyed, not only for Venus, but for all the other cases. It is frustrating not to know how the Babylonians regarded setting; however, by chance, the tablets give us a clue: setting is unfavourable and debilitating for the planet. These omens link the influence of the rising and the setting planets.

Here are two examples: 'If a child is born when Jupiter comes forth and Venus has set, it will go excellently with that man; his wife will leave (i.e., probably die before him)', and conversely: 'If a child is born when Venus comes forth and Jupiter has set, his wife will be stronger than he.' In other words, when rising, Venus (the wife) dominates Jupiter (the husband), who disappears into the setting mists.

Similar relations are established between Jupiter and Mars: 'If a child is born when Jupiter comes forth and Mars has set, it will go excellently with that man; he will see his personal enemy in defeat', and conversely: 'If a child is born when Mars comes forth and Jupiter has set, the hand of his personal enemy will capture him.' In other words, when rising, Mars (the aggressive enemy) vanquishes Jupiter (who often represents the king in these omens).

The meaning is clear: when a planet rises, it is strong and positive; when it sets, it loses its energy and becomes negative. These analogies have a certain astronomical logic. However, there is a disparity here between the Babylonian observations and my statistical own, which suggests that the setting planet is *also* in a zone of strong intensity, just as it is in the rising zone (see Figure 2, on p. 27). It is also regrettable that these last predictions have lost the 'psychological' aspect seen in the interpretations of rising planets.

It would be remarkable if, having given their attention to the rising and the setting of planets, the Babylonians also attached importance to one of the other Gauquelin 'plus zones': the culmination. Does the following tablet extract not, in fact, suggest that they did?: 'If a child is born when Jupiter is standing in the *tallu* . . .' (the rest of the prediction was obliterated]. And so on for the other planets. Here again, it is infuriating that the interpretations have disappeared in every case, for might this *tallu* not simply be the culmination? Unfortunately, this is not the case. We know from Van der Waerden (and Sachs confirms it) that: 'without any possible doubt *ziqpu* is the Babylonian term for culmination'.[11] (I refer the reader to the previous chapter.)

There is also a long list of birth omens which mention that the planets are 'in the *dur*', or 'in the *MI-SIR*'. This complicates things. Sachs makes the following comments about *tallu*, *dur*, *MI-SIR*: 'I do not know what the three possible phenomena are. *Tallu* points to a dividing line or cross-piece of some sort, *dur* may refer to a "bond", and as for *MI-SIR* I cannot offer even the faintest clue.'[12]

Whatever they are, none of the omens begins with: 'If a child is born when Jupiter [or whatever other planet] is standing in the

An Early 'Grain of Gold'?

ziqpu'; that is, none of them mentions the culmination. The Babylonians were very much aware of it but attached no predictive interest to it; for them, only the rising and setting (but also the *tallu*, the *dur*, the *MI-SIR*) were the bearers of omens.

In short, the most significant fact remains the Babylonian idea that the positions of planets in the diurnal movement are capable of exerting influence. On some (rare) occasions, my observations seem to confirm Babylonian predictions almost completely – when these link the rising of Mars to a 'hot temper', or that of Saturn to an 'obscure and constrained' existence, for example.

This might not amount to much, but is it not a wonder that, after the passage of twenty-five centuries, Babylonian omens and my statistics should be comparable? In my opinion, the Babylonians were at this point on the right track. These omens, according to Sachs, still only belong to a pre-horoscopic stage because 'all the phenomena can occur anywhere in the zodiac'. But that is precisely the point: my evidence regarding the effectiveness of the planets is *independent* of their zodiacal positions.

Unfortunately, the Babylonians were to commit a *fatal error in complicating the horoscope* from the moment that their astronomy allowed them to determine correctly the zodiacal signs. In henceforth giving the signs absolute primacy over the diurnal positions, they strayed from the truth and misled generations upon generations of astrologers. The Greeks, as I will show, tried to react, but only partially succeeded.

ACT THREE

Greek Astrology

6

THE FOUR PILLARS OF THE SKY

'Only a relatively crude horoscopic astrology has emerged from Babylonia. It is obvious that the non-Mesopotamian Hellenistic world made essential contributions to the more refined and expanded forms of horoscopic astrology,' remarks Sachs.[1] In fact, Greek astrology 'invented' almost all astrology that is in use today. Its influence first spread to Rome, and through Rome, to the whole world of antiquity.

Unlike its Babylonian predecessor, Greek astrology is well known. It has been the subject of numerous historical studies by Bouché-Leclercq,[2] Boll,[3] Cumont,[4] and Cramer,[5] to mention but a few. Numerous documents have been found, systematically studied and published, especially in Neugebauer and Van Hoesen's fundamental work, *Greek Horoscopes*.[6] Lastly, we have Greek astrological treatises, three of which are very famous: *Astronomicon*[7] by Manilius, *Tetrabiblos*[8] by Ptolemy, the most famous of all, since it was written by the most renowned astronomer of the time, and *Mathesis*[9] by Firmicus. These three works deal with so-called 'Greek' astrology, but it must be said that they were written in Roman times, in the first, the second and fourth centuries A.D., respectively. These various sources form the basis of the documentation for my search – in the extraordinarily complex field of the Greek horoscope – for 'precursory indications' of my observations. This is my goal: I am not writing a history of astrology, even less a treatise. Through necessity, I have made a *choice* and focused my attention on the points of doctrine which I regard as important from my point of view.

Why did the Greeks fall in love with Babylonian astrology as soon

Neo-Astrology

as they made contact with it, and to such an extent that the pupils quickly exceeded their teachers in their enthusiasm? Because their philosophy rendered them ripe to receive it.

The Greek Pythagoras, who lived in the sixth century B.C. was the first to explain systematically the concept of harmony of the world – this *harmonia* which requires that in nature 'everything be number', but a number structured according to *harmonia*. However, as Arthur Koestler remarks: 'It is not the pleasing effect of simultaneously sounded concordant strings . . . but something more austere.'[10]

Extended to the stars, the doctrine became the 'Harmony of the Spheres'. In the Pythagorean universe, the world is a sphere. Koestler continues:

> Around it the Sun, Moon, and the planets revolve in concentric circles, each fastened to a sphere or wheel. The swift revolution of each of these bodies causes a swish, or musical hum, in the air. Evidently each planet will hum at a different pitch, depending on the ratios of their respective orbits – just as the tone of a string depends on its length.[11]

Pythagoras's conception was to become a veritable astral religion. His influence on Plato's thought is obvious: the soul of man and the stars have the same immortal movement, and souls have a celestial origin. In *Timaeus*, as Louis Rougier noted:

> The rational soul of man is similar in all points to the soul of the world which merges with the heaven. Formed by the Demiurge of the same mixture, the rational soul is enclosed in the cranium, fashioned especially to receive it, in imitation of the vault of heaven.[12]

Formed from the same substance, the soul and the stars have also the same origin and the same destiny. The human soul is a 'spark of the astral substance'. Fallen from the stars, the soul returns there after our death.

The study of astronomy, the knowledge of astral influences, was the path to wisdom for the Pythagoreans, for whom 'the cosmic emotion which gave rise to the contemplation of starry skies was

The Four Pillars of the Sky

not Pascal's agony before the eternal silence of infinite space'.[13] This astral mysticism inspired Ptolemy, 'the prince of astrologers', to make the following proud profession of faith: 'Mortal as I am, I know that I am born for a day, but when I follow the serried multitude of the stars in their circular course, my feet no longer touch the earth; I ascend to Zeus himself to feast me on ambrosia, the food of the gods.'[14]

Deep affinities also linked the Babylonian doctrines with the philosophical school of Stoicism, whose influence was widespread among Greek thinkers. Franz Cumont asserts: 'Stoicism conceived the world as a great organism, the "sympathetic" forces of which acted and re-acted necessarily upon one another, and was bound in consequence to attribute a predominating influence to the celestial bodies, the greatest and the most powerful of all in nature.'[15]

'As above so below.' This famous expression has been attributed to the legendary Hermes Trismegistus, which literally means 'Hermes three times great'. In other words, man is a microcosm, the heavens a macrocosm. Between them exists a current of universal sympathy. The hermetic tradition was born in Greece, which was ready to accept astrology and to develop the theory of the horoscope based on the zodiac as delineated by the Babylonians.

One of the most important innovations of the Greek astrologers was the calculation of the point of Ascendant – called *'horoscopos'* in that period, which literally means: 'watcher of the hour'. Because the Earth turns on its axis in twenty-four hours, the Ascendant quickly passes through the twelve signs of the zodiacal belt, completing its round in one day. From this comes the necessity of 'watching the hour', that is, of knowing the precise instant of a child's birth, in order to determine its Ascendant. When we know the time of birth and the Ascendant, we can then calculate the positions of the Sun, the Moon and planets in the sky during the twenty-four-hour movement, according to the horizon and the meridian of the place of birth.

Very quickly – and this fact was to be repeated *ad nauseam* in astrological treatises – particular importance was attached to the 'angles' in the sky, or 'centres'. 'The "centres" are the four points at which the ecliptic (middle of the zodiac) meets with the horizon and the meridian at a given moment. Consequently, these points are the rising and the setting points, and the points of upper and lower culmination.'[16] The rising point is called the Ascendant; the upper culmination is the Midheaven; the setting point is the Descendant; the lower culmination is the imum coeli. As we have seen before, these terms and their abbreviations are still in use today (see Figure 1, on p. 14). Taking this structure as their starting point, the Greeks divided the sky into twelve zones which they called 'houses'. But the twelve 'houses' did not appear immediately. Their introduction into the Greek horoscope was gradual. This evolution and also the importance attributed to the centres, can be perceived when comparing two horoscopes published by Neugebauer and Van Hoesen. In both cases the authors provide the original representation in Greek.[17]

Figure 5 is the graphic representation of the horoscope for a birth on 29 September, in A.D. 15 'at the fourth hour of the night'. We realize the importance of angles through the drawing of a cross which divides the horoscope into four quarters. The text says: 'Taurus is the Horoscopus [Ascendant], house of Venus . . . Scorpio is setting, house of Mars . . . lower Midheaven in Leo . . .' The whole still appears primitive.

Let us compare it with Figure 6, the horoscope of a much later birth, on 28 October, in A.D. 497, about 500 years after the first. On this occasion, the houses are clearly indicated even though the diagram seems to give more prominence to the four heavenly angles (in fact, these are the four houses which are called 'angular'). The evolution at the time towards a horoscope of greater complexity was a fact, if not a good thing.

In *Astronomicon*, Manilius, who was also a poet – it is written in verse – describes the four heavenly angles with an evocative talent:

> Come now, prepare an attentive mind for learning the cardinal points: four in all; they have positions in the firmament permanently fixed and receive in succession the speeding signs. One looks out from the rising of the heavens as they are born into the world, and has the first view of the Earth from the level horizon; the second

The Four Pillars of the Sky

[Μ]ΕϹΟΥΡ̂
ΥΔΡΟΧΟΩ
ΙΧΘΥΕϹ ΑΙΓΟ
ΚΡΙΟϹ ΤΟΞΟΤΗϹ ΚΡΟΝΟϹ
ϹΕΛΗΝ ΩΡΟϹΚΟ — ΤΑΥΡΟϹ — [ϹΚΟΡΠΙ] ΕΡΜΗϹ
ΔΙΔΥΜΟΙ ΖΥΓΟϹ / ΗΛΙΟϹ ΑΡΗϹ
ΚΑΡΚΙΝΟϹ ΠΑΡΘΕΝΟϹ
ΛΕΩΝ
ΥΠΟΓΗΝ

Figure 5: The four angles of the Greek horoscope (A.D. 15): Horoscope corresponding to a birth on 29 September. If we compare this still primitive horoscope with the one in Figure 6 drawn almost 500 years later, we observe a trend towards greater complexity in the horoscope.

---

faces it from the opposite edge of the sky, the point from which the starry sphere retires and hurtles headlong into Tartarus; a third marks the zenith of high heaven, where wearied Phoebus halts with panting steeds and rests the day and determines the mid-point of shadows; the fourth occupies their descent and commences their return, and at equal distances it beholds their risings and settings. These points are charged with exceptional powers, and the influence they exert on fate is the greatest known to our science, because the celestial circle is totally held in position by them as by eternal supports; did they not receive the circle, sign after sign in succession ... heaven would fly apart and its fabric disintegrate and perish.[18]

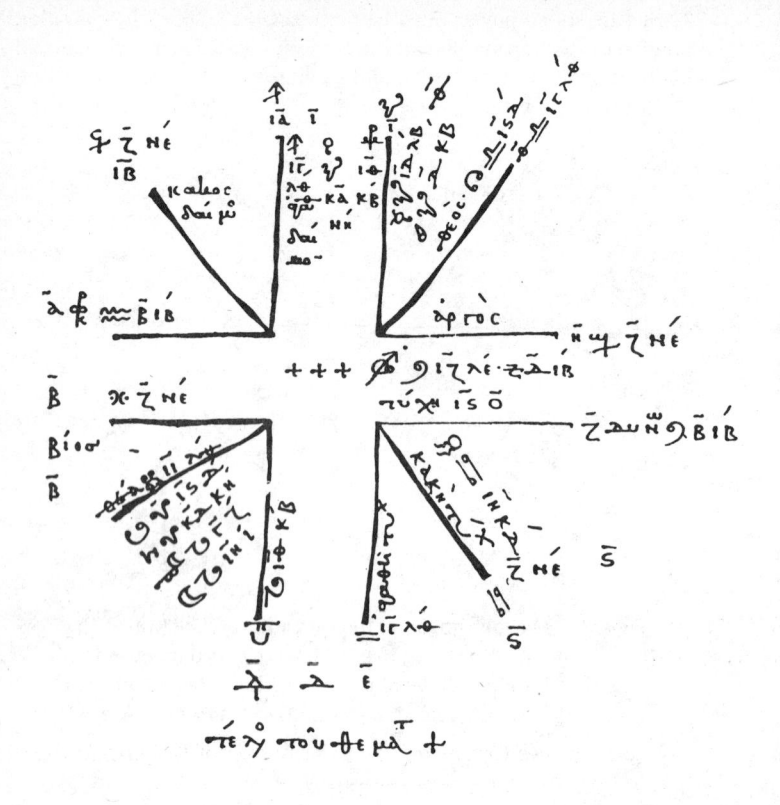

Figure 6: The four angles of the Greek horoscope (A.D. 497):
Horoscope corresponding to a birth on 28 October. We notice
a great enrichment of astrological factors but the angles are
still predominant.

Through his poetic imagination, the astrologer only expresses belief in the power of the centres, and thus the dominance of the stars which are positioned there at the moment of birth. In *Tetrabiblos*, Ptolemy confirms this in less romantic terms:

The Four Pillars of the Sky

> Their [the stars'] power must be determined ... from their position relative to the horizon; for they are most powerful when they are in Midheaven or approaching it, and second when they are exactly on the horizon or in the succedent place; their power is greater when they are in the orient, and less when they culminate beneath the Earth.[19]

When reading this, we are struck by the agreement – at least approximate – between the four angles of the sky and the four Gauquelin 'plus zones' which are positioned just after the rising, the upper culmination, the setting and lower culmination (see Figure 2, on p. 27).

It was certainly the Greeks who invented the notion of the four angles in the horoscope. As I showed in the previous chapter, none of the Babylonian horoscopes included the Ascendant point, from which angle the other three are calculated.

Thus the Greeks did better than the Babylonians, and it seems reasonable to consider this notion of angles in the horoscope as a fruitful idea heralding certain neo-astrological observations. The Greeks figure here as forerunners. But to what extent? For the Greeks, if I may say so, did get carried away and passed by the true interpretation of the phenomena.

In my opinion, the Greeks erred not only by not keeping to the idea of four angles, but also by dividing the sky into twelve houses and then attributing arbitrary influences to them. In the preceding chapter, which is devoted to the horoscope, I briefly explained what the twelve houses are and their significance. I shall not return to this subject in detail, but only present here two Latin lines, which sum it up, and which have served for generations of astrologers as a mnemonic. They are quoted in the *Epitome*:

> *Vita, Lucrum, Frates, Genitor, Nati ac Valetudo*
> *Uxor, Mors, Iter, et Regnum, Benefactaque, Carcer.*[20]
>
> [Life, Gain, Brothers, Father, Children and Health,
> Spouse, Death, Travels, Empire, Kindness and Prison.]

Neo-Astrology

Greek astrology also established a hierarchy of power for these twelve Houses: the angular houses are houses I, IV, VII and X because they precede the angles; the succedent houses are houses II, V, VIII and XI because they follow the angular houses; the cadent houses are houses III, VI, IX and XII because they have already passed an angle.

The angular houses are the most powerful and the cadent houses the weakest. The former are also the best, and the latter the least good. The hierarchy and value of the houses are often justified by poetic-scientific analogies. Manilius affirms:

> The temple that is immediately above the Horoscope and is the next but one to heaven's zenith [house XII] is a temple of ill omen, hostile to future activity and all too fruitful of bane; nor that alone, but like unto it will prove the abode which with confronting star shines below the occident and adjacent to it. And so that this temple should not outdo the former, each alike moves dejected from a cardinal point with a spectacle of ruin before its eyes. Each shall be a portal of toil: in one you are doomed to climb, in the other to fall.[21]

It must be said in passing that it is a strange logic to regard both as weak and unlucky house XII, which rises on the horizon, because it must 'always climb', and house VI, positioned in the setting, because, also according to Manilius, it 'always falls under the horizon'. Manilius speaks of houses as if they were human beings and not mathematical conventions.

Is the system of astrological houses a valid forerunner of the Gauquelin 'plus zones'? I have mentioned all that I think is good in the Greek notion of angles. But, as far as the houses go, my answer is that neither the intensity nor the signification of the houses has been borne out by my observations:

- the intensity of the twelve houses. For me, the zones of maximum influence for a planet are found for the most part after the horizon and meridian. These zones correspond on the whole to houses XII, IX, VI and III. The Greeks called these areas of the sky 'cadent houses' (from the Latin

The Four Pillars of the Sky

cadere – to fall), and claimed that stars in them could only have a weakened influence, seen as inauspicious;
– the signification of the twelve houses. The appointed destiny which the Greeks attributed to houses XII, IX, VI and III, has nothing to do with my observations. Here is an extract from the list on p. 19: 'House III: brothers and sisters, short journeys . . . House VI: work, employees, small animals . . . House IX: long journeys, religion, philosophy . . . House XII: ordeals, chronic illness, prison.'

The contradiction between the bad influences attributed to house XII and my results is striking: a large number of subjects who have achieved great success were born when planets were positioned in this part of the sky. The signification of the three other cadent houses does not appear to fit in any better with my observations.

Why did the Greeks divide the diurnal movement into twelve houses and why did they number them in the *opposite* direction to that of the actual movement of the Sun and planets during the day? Because they followed a double analogy in the zodiac. They regarded as astrologically extremely important the twelve signs of the zodiac as defined by the Babylonians. However, whereas in the zodiac the real movement of the stars is in the *opposite* direction to that of the hands of a clock, in their daily movement, the stars follow a clockwise direction. The famous Greek logic was thus hoist by its own petard.

It would have been more logical to number the houses following the true astronomical direction. Starting from the Ascendant, house XII would become house I, house XI house II, and so on, in keeping with the Sun which rises, climbs the sky, reaches its culmination at midday and sets, and in keeping also with the succession of the hours.

Would the historical course of astrology have been different if the Greek astrologers, instead of numbering the houses in the 'wrong direction', had numbered them in the 'right' one? No, because they would have retained the structure of twelve distinct zones of influ-

Neo-Astrology

ence, and each house would have kept – whichever way it had been numbered – a clearly defined astrological meaning.

The main error – in the cold light of my statistical observations – was to invent the twelve houses at all; in comparison, the numbering of the houses in the opposite direction to that of the astronomical movement is only a secondary mistake.

The inventor of the houses is not known. They probably were a gradual, collective creation. In any case, it was not Ptolemy, for all his fame. In *Tetrabiblos*, he took the houses into account, but did not lay much emphasis on their importance, contrarily to Manilius in his *Astronomicon*. Ptolemy was more of an astronomer than an astrologer, but certain horoscopic rules must have worked upon his unconscious mind: Is it not strange that house XII, the house that contains the rising of the Sun and planets should be regarded as 'weak'? This problem perplexed him, especially when he described the laws governing the power of the planets at birth.

Thus, he proposed a slight amendment: 'In the first place we must consider ... the twelfth part of the zodiac surrounding the Horoscope [Ascendant], from 5 degrees above the actual horizon up to the 25 degrees that remain, which is rising in succession to the horizon.'[22] In other words, the planet that is *physically* positioned in house XII, but in the 5 degrees above its rising point, should in fact be *technically* considered as still in cardinal house I, i.e. as dominant. However, Ptolemy stresses that this is only true for 5 degrees: after that the planet really falls into house XII, 'the house of the Evil Daemon'[23] where 'the thick, misty exhalation from the moisture of the earth'[24] rules as master.

This shift of 5 degrees around the rising point is accepted by many astrologers, including contemporary authors, who are exegetes of my work. Nevertheless, Ptolemy was far from drawing the obvious conclusion from the problems posed by house XII; which would have led to the abandonment, pure and simple of the system of houses. In his *Horoscopes and History*, J. D. North makes an interesting remark:

> The usual way of approaching the historical problem, namely through astrological handbooks, can give a very misleading idea of

actual practice, as may be seen from a study of the examples of Greek horoscopes provided by Neugebauer and Van Hoesen. Out of 168 horoscopes, from a period of nearly seven centuries (71 B.C. to A.D. 621), only twenty-seven give an indication of both the Ascendant and either Midheaven or Lower Midheaven. Of these, only *two* include the limits of the twelve houses (*loci*).[25]

Was Ptolemy's *Tetrabiblos* then too scholarly for the majority of practitioners, deterred by the technical difficulties of calculating the houses? North thinks otherwise: 'It seems that Greek astrologers did not attach such importance to the houses as later Islamic and Christian astrologers were to do.'[26] Whatever the case may be, the theory of the four angles of the sky, like the system of houses, remained typically Greek inventions – the former, for the better, and the latter for the worse.

7

ASTRAL PSYCHOLOGY

In the horoscope, the division of the sky – the angles, the houses – is only a backdrop without a cast. It is the Sun, the Moon, the planets which enliven the setting, give it colour, soul. The Greeks knew very little about the planets before making the acquaintance of the Babylonians. They were amazing theoreticians, but poor observers. Franz Cumont comments:

> When the Greeks learnt to recognize the five planets known in antiquity, they gave them names derived from their character. Venus, whose brightness Homer had already celebrated, was called 'Herald of the Dawn' or 'Herald of Light', or on the other hand 'Vespertine', according to whether she was considered as the star of the morning or that of the evening (the identity of these two being not yet recognized). Mercury was named the 'Twinkling Star', Mars, because of his red colour, the 'Fiery Star', Jupiter the 'Luminous Star', Saturn the 'Brilliant Star'.[1]

None of this is astrological; it simply resembles a primitive astronomical nomenclature, which does neither attribute influences to these planets, nor make them divine residences. The astrology of planetary gods is a Babylonian idea, but the Greeks quickly adopted it. To quote Cumont again:

> After the fourth century other titles are found to supersede these ancient names, which are gradually ousted from use. The planets become the stars of Hermes, Aphrodite, Ares, Zeus, Kronos. This seems due to the fact that in Babylonia these same planets were dedicated respectively to Nebo, Ishtar, Nergal, Marduk and Ninib. In accordance with the usual procedure of the ancients, the Greeks substituted for these barbarous divinities those of their own deities who bore some resemblance to them.[2]

To Jupiter-Marduk, the most powerful Babylonian divinity, the Greeks assigned Zeus, the king of gods, 'whose golden light burns most steadily in the sky'. To Mars-Nergal, the master of war, they assigned Ares, because of its red colour which recalls the blood of battlefields, etc. Cumont continues:

> Clearly, the ideas of Babylonian star-worship have come here, for the ancient mythology of Hellas did not put the stars under the patronage of the Olympians nor establish any connection between them. Thus the names of planets, which we employ today, are an English translation of a Latin translation of a Greek translation of Babylonian nomenclature.[3]

The planetary gods are more powerful than the gods of Olympus or the saints in Heaven, according to Cumont: 'To each was attached a planet, a metal, a stone. Each presided over a period of life, a portion of the body, and a faculty of the soul.'[4] The soul is a particle detached from the planets. The warmth which gives life to the human microcosm comes from it. With our first breath at birth, it marks us with a permanent stamp. This is the origin of the theory of 'astral signatures'.

In fact, the Greeks did not regard the 'planetary soul' as a purely religious concept, they gave it a psychological anchor. 'The planets,' writes J. C. Eade, 'are considered to have a "complexion" that imparts to the individual his "temperament".'[5] The influence of the work of Hippocrates (c. 460–377 B.C.) on the subject of temperament and illness, taken up and further developed by the Greek physician, Galen (c. 130–200), can be seen here.[6]

Notions of individual temperament, of psychological personality, were the most revolutionary to be developed by the Greeks. In a word, *the Greeks simply invented astral psychology*. The psychologist Simon Kemp writes in a recent article:

> For both writers [Ptolemy and Firmicus] each planet produced different personality traits. This is most clearly seen in the traits associated with the ruling planet, which was ascertained by a variety of astronomical formulae. Thus, Ptolemy described Jupiter as making people 'magnanimous, generous, god-fearing, honourable, pleasure-

Neo-Astrology

loving, kind, with qualities of leadership', while Mercury produces people who are 'wise, shrewd, thoughtful, learned, inventive, inquirers into nature, speculative, gifted, emulous, successful in attaining their ends'. Firmicus's descriptions are quite similar: 'Those who have Jupiter as ruler of the chart are always trustworthy, of high spirits, and are impelled toward great deeds ... commanding in all their acts, noble, famous, honourable, lovers of luxury, cheerful, desiring to please in every way ... Those who have Mercury as ruler of the chart are clever, talented, students of all things, modest; they desire to learn the secret of all skills.'[7]

Kemp draws a logical conclusion from this:

> The fact that the ancient astrological account of personality derived from astrological theory had implications for the ideas about personality produced in it. First, the astrological theory of personality had to be a trait theory; this followed naturally because there were only seven planets known, and hence seven dimensions of personality.[8]

To describe the character of a person in terms of traits of personality is an approach currently employed by psychologists. I also started out from these same general principles, when I formulated the 'method of traits of character' (see chapter 2). Having compiled the traits of character of subjects from their biographies, I compared them to the position of planets at the hour of birth, and, finally, I derived the descriptions of planetary psychological types.

On the whole, all I did was to check the Greek innovation of planetary dimensions of the personality. But do my observations tally with those of Greek and Roman astrologers? Again this raises the question of how far we should give credit to the forerunners of neo-astrology. To attempt a reply, the best thing is to refer to the great classical works of Manilius, Ptolemy and Firmicus.

In his *Astronomicon*, Manilius omitted to include a chapter on planets (or else, a chapter has been lost), while concentrating at length on the signs of the zodiac and on the houses. In any case, he is of no use to me here. On the other hand, Ptolemy's *Tetrabiblos* and Firmicus's *Mathesis* are very informative, each explaining how the planets affect the personality. The great difficulty in studying their books in order to extract the planetary types in the modern way, however, is the abundance of interposed notions which clutter up the issue, as for example the notions of *favourable* and *unfavourable*. In the writings of these authors, there are always the 'good guys' and the 'bad buys'. Jupiter and Venus are regarded as 'beneficial', Mars and Saturn as 'malefic'. Moreover, as the Greek horoscope is of considerable complexity, it sometimes happens that the 'beneficial' are no longer so if they are 'badly placed', positioned in a zodiacal sign which does not 'suit them', etc. Conversely, the 'malefic' planets can appear, in certain circumstances, to be reasonably inoffensive.

This perpetual interaction of factors gives a *splintered* image of each planetary type which has to be reconstructed through the numerous chapters of these books. This leaves, of course, too much to interpretation: by taking a quote from Ptolemy or Firmicus 'out of context', I can easily ridicule these authors and declare that they were wrong; equally, the choice of another quotation 'out of context' makes them appear to assert truths they did not really support. I will give an example of how difficult it is to remain objective by taking a *simple* case (of course, the choice of the example is already mine, implying the adoption of a position).

In Book III of Ptolemy's *Tetrabiblos*, there is a long chapter – chapter 13 – called 'Of the Quality of the Soul', that I have read and re-read over the years. I have even included it as an appendix to my work, *La Cosmopsychologie*[9] (Cosmopsychology), so that the reader could judge it on its own merits. Every time I consult this piece again, I experience a number of feelings: first excitement, then frustration, and, in the end, irritation. It is infuriating not to be able to know with certainty whether this text is indeed a precursor to my observations on the traits of character. However, it is best to let Ptolemy speak for himself. He begins his chapter with the planet Saturn:

> If Saturn alone is ruler of the soul and dominates Mercury and the Moon, if he has a dignified position with reference to the universe

and the angles, he makes his subjects lovers of the body, strong-minded, deep thinkers, lovers of property, avaricious, violent, amassing treasure and jealous; but if his position is the opposite and without dignity, he makes them sordid, petty, mean-spirited, indifferent, mean-minded, malignant, cowardly, diffident, evil-speakers, solitary, tearful, shameless, superstitious, fond of toil, unfeeling, devisers of plots against their friends, gloomy, taking no care of the body.[10]

Let us now follow in with what Firmicus writes in Chapter XIX of his treatise, *Mathesis*, about the same planet:

> If Saturn is the ruler of the chart, is favourably located, and has been allotted the rulership by the waxing Moon, he will make the natives proud, arrogant, honoured, respectable, serious, of good counsel. Their work is respected in judgement and they fulfil all their duties correctly and prudently. They will, however, always be at odds with wife and children. They will be distant, not much occupied with self; taking little food but enjoying drink. These men are of moderate size, pale, sluggish; they will have stomach trouble and vomit easily, be attacked by malignant humours, and be constantly a prey to internal pains. They will be malevolent, anxious, hard-working, troubled in mind; always making a living connection with water.[11]

There is, for sure, a family resemblance between these two portraits, aside from the discrepancies of detail although two centuries separate Ptolemy and Firmicus. The attributes of Saturn thus appear to stem from a long-standing tradition whose origin, no doubt, goes back to the Babylonians. (I refer the reader to the Babylonian omen which says: 'If a child is born when Saturn comes forth, then his life will be dark, obscure, sick, and constrained.')

Nevertheless, continuity does not necessarily mean validity. Without further comment for the moment, I will list here twenty traits of character linked with the presence of the planet Saturn at birth in the Gauquelin 'plus zones' (taken from Table 2, on p. 29): 'cold, concentrated, conscientious, discreet, introvert, methodical, meticulous, modest, observant, precise, reserved, sad, simple, sombre, stiff, taciturn, thoughtful, timid, uncommunicative, wise.'

Astral Psychology

With these elements of response in hand, a word-for-word reading of Ptolemy and Firmicus appears to show that they correctly stressed both the serious and sombre sides of Saturn. Ptolemy talks of : 'deep thinkers ... austere ... of a single purpose ... laborious ... diffident ... solitary ... gloomy.' Firmicus writes: 'honoured, respectable, serious ... fulfil their duties correctly and prudently ... distant, anxious.'[12] On the other hand, Ptolemy talks of the Saturnian as: 'dictatorial, violent, sordid, petty, mean-minded [etc.]' where Firmicus writes: 'proud, arrogant ... enjoying drink ... malevolent [etc.]'.[13] There are two ways of being Saturnian according to these authors: the 'good' and the 'bad'. Indeed, only the 'good' way bears similarity to my observations.

Anyone who is set against neo-astrology will see in my analysis only chance and hair-splitting. This hypothesis is not to be rejected. For my part, I believe that the Greeks were on the right track when they created astral psychology. However, although their idea of attributing traits of character to planets was pure genius, it was still too hazy to be able to progress much further.

As astrology diversified, expanding to cover the whole of the vast Roman Empire, astrologers endeavoured to improve their practice in a strictly experimental spirit. An interesting concrete example of their attitude that was saved from destruction was recently revealed in detail thanks to the work of Neugebauer and Van Hoesen. It is *Anthology*, by the Roman Vettius Valens, a practising astrologer and forerunner of astrological research who lived in the second century A.D. Neugebauer and Van Hoesen comment:

> The importance of the *Anthology* of Vettius Valens can be illustrated by the following figures. With its about 130 (partial or complete) horoscopes it contains twice as many examples of Greek horoscopes as all papyri combined. Without Vettius Valens (whose examples range from A.D. 37 to 188) we should have only five examples of 'literary' horoscopes before A.D. 380.[14]

Referring to *Anthology* in 1899, the historian Bouché-Leclercq wrote in his *Greek Astrology*: 'I attempted to make the most use of this work ... which is mostly unintelligible.'[15] But Neugebauer and Van Hoesen retort:

Only a prolonged and detailed study will lead to a better understanding of the text, its composition, and its – undoubtedly great – influence upon later treatises ... All horoscopes in Vettius Valens serve a specific purpose, namely to provide examples for certain doctrines which are discussed in the main body of the work. A priori it would be perfectly permissible to assume that such examples were arbitrarily made up in order to demonstrate by concrete configuration how conclusions should be drawn from them according to theory ... (but) the fact that every one of these horoscopes can be shown to be astronomically correct for a date in the first or second century A.D. is therefore proof that Vettius Valens was using empirical material exclusively, collected either by himself or by his predecessors. ... Thus, during these years, Vettius Valens himself was *systematically collecting and analyzing a large amount of statistical material of birth data, life histories, and deaths in order to confirm or modify the theoretical structure of astrology* [my emphasis]. This shows that Hellenistic-Roman astrology was still under development near the end of the second century.[14]

The term 'statistical material' does not strictly conform to what the specialists today call statistical research. But there was a scientific approach in Valens's intentions and there must have been other Vettius Valenses whose works have been lost. His undeniable merit is to have preserved for us the horoscope of the Emperor Hadrian, born in Italica, near Seville in Spain, on 24 January, in A.D. 76. Neugebauer and Van Hoesen included this horoscope in their work,[17] and I have reproduced it here (see Figure 7). This is an interesting horoscope: Was not the Emperor Hadrian born at the moment when Jupiter and the Moon were rising on the horizon of Italica in the early hours of 24 January, in A.D. 76? In Table 1 (see p. 25), I showed that politicians tended to be born under such a configuration. I am not taken in by this 'suggestive' example. It is only an anecdote, but I find it exciting. Moreover, Vettius Valens would not have agreed with my interpretation. He gives of Hadrian's horoscope a very different explanation, which I shall charitably refrain from publishing.[18] But, to be fair, it may have been difficult for him, in spite of his collection of over a hundred cases, to do any better, just as Hadrian's personal doctor was unable to treat the

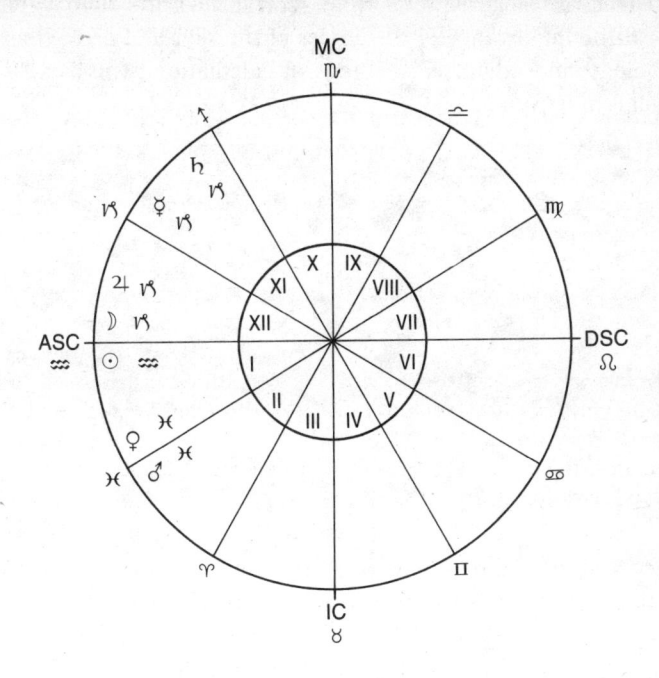

Figure 7: Horoscope of the Roman Emperor Hadrian:*
Taken from the collection of the Roman astrologer Vettius
Valens; note that the planets Uranus, Neptune and Pluto were
not known in antiquity.
* Born in Italica, near Seville (Spain), on 24 January, A.D. 76,
at sunrise.

'dropsy of the heart'[19] from which the emperor was suffering until the age of 63, when he died in great agony.

The Babylonians bequeathed a tentative doctrine to the Greeks. The Greeks and the Romans made a grandiose concept out of it. They made many mistakes regarding the role of the zodiac, the houses, and the aspects, on which it is better not to dwell. Nevertheless, Greek astrology showed the importance of the time of birth, stressed the importance of the angles of the sky, and created astral psychology and advanced methods of calculation. This is all that we will retain from it.

Second Interlude:

KEPLER: ASTRONOMER, ASTROLOGER

'The Renaissance saw no contradiction between astrology and science; rather the dominion of the heavenly bodies over all earthly things was viewed by some as the natural law *par excellence*, the law which assures the regularity of phenomena,' writes Jean Seznec in his book *The Survival of the Pagan Gods*.[1] In the Middle Ages, the ideas of Ptolemy were preserved by Arab scholars, who translated all his works in the ninth century. The first Latin translation was published by the famous erudite Gérard de Crémone in 1175. From then on, a larger number of editions of the works of Ptolemy and other antiquity writers were published during the Renaissance. But, in the darkest Middle Ages and under the domination of the Catholic Church, astrology never really disappeared from western Europe. To quote Seznec again:

> As the Middle Ages and the Renaissance come to be better known, the traditional antithesis between them grows less marked. The medieval period appears 'less dark and static', and the Renaissance 'less bright and less sudden'. Above all, it is now recognized that pagan antiquity, far from experiencing a 'rebirth' in fifteenth-century Italy, had remained alive within the culture and the art of the Middle Ages. Even the gods were not *restored* to life, for they had never disappeared from the memory or imagination of man.[2]

Thanks to certain authors, such as Marsilio Ficino (1433–99), the hermetic-occult tradition proved to be a living force of the Renaissance. The work of Cornelius Agrippa (1486–1535), *De Occulta Philosophia*, which so profoundly influenced Kepler, is partly dedicated to astral magic, or how to attract and use the influence of the stars. Agrippa was inspired by Ficino, who in turn claims to have been initiated by the Egyptian sage, Hermes Trismegistus.

Neo-Astrology

In the Renaissance, this hermetism, this astral magic, went hand in hand with the beginnings of modern scientific thought. There was no contradiction there for the great authors of the time. More than anywhere else, this dualism is alive in the work of Johannes Kepler (1571–1630), the astronomer-astrologer.

> In Kepler, there is an exact reciprocity in the status of astronomy and of astrology: they are conceived according to the same model, where nature serves as a mediator between the two extremes which are God and men ... He keeps astrology alive because it is the structural doublet of astronomy, because it is, in a way, its profane image ... [Through Kepler's work and thought] we see that, no more than the Copernican revolution, the introduction of mathematics as the norm of knowledge did not serve to discredit astrology, nor to found a new scientific spirit; quite to the contrary. The upheavals would come fast, but later. The old order continued; and Kepler's ambition was to gain the title which his contemporaries conferred on Copernicus, when they called him the new Ptolemy; but not only by transforming the latter's *Almagest*, but also by renewing his *Tetrabiblos*.[3]

These comments by Gérard Simon indicate in themselves the degree to which Kepler's role is central in my book. This merits our attention for a few moments.

In February 1967, I went to visit the house where Kepler was born, in Weil-der-Stadt, a small town in Württemberg, provincially sleepy in winter. It was a very small, slightly lop-sided house, almost a doll's house, carefully painted white, with crisscrossed beams. The house looked on to the main square, with a red-stone fountain in the centre – a hexagonal fountain, no doubt in honour of Kepler who was so fascinated by geometrical forms. The door to the house was closed and there were no other visitors. Hesitantly, I rang the bell and the keeper soon arrived, but with measured steps, like a Württemberg peasant crossing his field. We mounted a spiral staircase, narrow and short. The keeper showed me the room where Kepler was born, and the wooden cradle, witness of his first wails. Then I passed into a slightly larger room with a low ceiling, the small museum with astrolabes and some manuscripts. For the education of the rare visitors, there is a detailed explanation of the

Second Interlude: Kepler: Astronomer, Astrologer

astronomical laws discovered by the child of Weil-der-Stadt. There is not much on astrology: a few prints hidden in dark corners.

I had to collect myself for a few moments, moved despite everything. Then I bought a few dull postcards and departed through the narrow, deserted streets of the little town for my rustic inn, where the morning smelled of good, piping-hot coffee and blueberry jam. I owed this pilgrimage to myself.

Johannes Kepler is considered by contemporary astronomers as the epitome of a man of science. He was a scientific genius for sure, discoverer of the three laws of planetary movement which carry his name. But Kepler also dedicated his life to the Pythagorean theory of the harmony of the spheres, according to which each orbiting planet emits a different music or sound. It was because of this *idée fixe*, coupled with his tireless patience and his mathematical genius, that he succeeded in setting out his famous laws.

When only twenty-five, in 1596, Kepler published in Tübingen his *Mysterium Cosmographicum*, in which he asserted that each planetary sphere was inscribed within a perfect solid. In the orbit or sphere of Saturn, he inscribed a cube and in that cube another sphere, that of Jupiter. Mars was, according to him, inscribed in a pyramid, delimited by four equilateral angles; between the spheres of Mars and the Earth, there was a dodecahedron (twelve plane faces) inserted; between the spheres of Mars and Venus, an icosahedron (twenty equilateral triangles). Arthur Koestler states: 'They were also called the "Pythagorean" or "Platonic" solids. Being perfectly symmetrical, each can be inscribed into a sphere, so that all its vertices (corners) lie on the surface of the sphere.'[4]

This idea of Kepler's was wrong. He himself would later demonstrate that the path followed by the planets was not a circle but an ellipse, that the space occupied by the trajectory of these stars was not inscribed in perfect circles, but in types of geometrically variable ovoid forms. Kepler openly admitted his error in a later edition of *Mysterium Cosmographicum* published twenty-five years on. On the other hand, his belief in a 'Pythagorean' astrology was never abandoned, as is illustrated in *Tertius Interveniens*, one of his last works: 'The natural soul of a man is not larger than a single point;

Neo-Astrology

and upon these points the shape and character of the whole heaven, be it a hundred times as large as it is, are imprinted *potentialiter*.'[5] It is in this book and in *Harmonices Mundi* (The Harmonies of the Universe), so Pythagorean a title, that Kepler clearly revealed his mind.

Wolfgang Pauli, Nobel Prize winner for physics for 1945, analysing Kepler's ideas, wonders how Kepler managed to integrate his own astrology, 'so different to the usual form that we know', into a general system of ideas on the natural sciences. He writes:

> According to Kepler, the individual soul, which he calls *vis formatrix* or *matrix formativa*, possesses the fundamental ability to react with the help of the *instinctus* to certain harmonious proportions which correspond to specific rational divisions of the circle. In music this intellectual power reveals itself in the perception of euphony (consonance) in certain musical intervals, an effect that Kepler thus does not explain in a purely mechanical way. Now the soul is said to have a similar reactibility to the numerous proportions of the angles which the *rays* of stellar light, striking the earth, form with each other. It is with these, in Kepler's opinion, that astrology should concern itself ... Acording to him, then, the stars exert no special remote influence, since their true distances are of no importance to astrology and only their light rays can be regarded as effective. The soul knows about the harmonious proportions through the *instinctus* without conscious reflection because the soul, by virtue of its circular form, is an image of God in Whom these proportions and the geometric truths following therefrom exist from all eternity. Now since the soul, in consequence of its circular form, has knowledge of these, it is impressed by external forms of the configurations of rays and retains a memory of them from its very birth ... The soul, according to Kepler, contains the idea of the zodiac within itself by virtue of its inherent circular form; but it is the planets, and not the fixed stars, which (through the intermediary of light) are the effective vehicles of astrological influence. The 'distribution of the twelve signs among the seven planets' is for him a fable.[6]

On the other hand, Kepler believed in the importance of what he called 'aspect', a harmonious combination of two astral rays. He explains in *Harmonices Mundi*:

Second Interlude: Kepler: Astronomer, Astrologer

> The soul contains within itself the idea of the zodiac. It can therefore tell if a particular planet is positioned at a precise moment at a precise degree of this zodiac, and measure the angles of the rays which converge on the Earth; and as it also receives the 'irradiation' of the Divine Essence of geometrical figures . . . it can work out the distance between angles and judge if they are harmonious or otherwise . . . The human soul is moulded at birth into a pre-existing form which is formed on Earth by the luminous rays which come from the stars.[7]

The angles at which two stars give out rays are especially important if they are inscribed in the circle to form simple geometrical forms: triangles, squares, hexagons, perfect images of the *anima mundi* to which the human soul reacts as a cosmic resonator. Elsewhere, Kepler also affirms: 'Nothing can exist or happen under the visible sky, which is not felt in some hidden way by the faculties of the Earth and Nature: faculties of the mind on this Earth are affected as much as the heavens themselves are.'[8]

It is not, in fact, the case that the human soul and the heavens maintain mysterious harmonies between them: the Earth is here the indispensable catalyst. As C. G. Jung notes:

> Kepler supposes that the secret of the marvellous correspondence is to be found in the *earth*, because the earth is animated by an *anima telluris*, for whose existence he adduces a number of proofs. Among these are: the constant temperature below the surface of the earth; the peculiar power of the earth-soul to produce metals, minerals and fossils, namely the *facultas formatrix*, which is similar to that of the womb. [That is, similar to what a mother's breast can accomplish while she awaits the birth of a child.] . . . The seat of astrological synchronicity is not in the planets but in the earth; not in matter, but in the *anima telluris.* Therefore every kind of natural or living power in bodies has a certain 'divine similitude'.[9]

When reading Kepler's ideas on the Soul-Earth-Cosmos relationship, we realize that he believes in astrology, but is against the classical horoscope. He criticized tradition and often adopted unorthodox stands, but nevertheless, he had a deep conviction that astrology – like astronomy – needed to be reformulated in order to become a

Neo-Astrology

true scientific doctrine. This, for him, was the case with the twelve houses, for example. To quote Simon on the subject:

> He completely rejects, without even considering that a real discussion is needed, the division of the sky into astrological houses; too clearly, the method and norms of interpretation are of anthropological origin, and have no foundation in the nature of things.[10]

For himself Kepler asserts: 'Astrologers have adopted the division into twelve houses to be able to supply clear answers to everything man wants to know. But I believe this procedure to be impossible, superstitious, suitable for fortune-tellers.'[11] Simon adds to this:

> We must note that Kepler does not refuse to consider *all* the elements of the classical horoscope: he retains those which appear to possess a natural efficacy. He attributes importance to the cardinal houses, which contain the Ascendant, the Midheaven, the Western Pole, and the *imum coeli* because the planets found in these privileged positions, or in an aspect with them, affect the soul of the new-born child more strongly than when they are in other positions.[12]

To David Fabricius, who reproaches him for having kept only the four cardinal houses, Kepler replies: 'Demonstrate the old houses to me. Explain their number; prove that there can be neither fewer nor more; from the very archetype of the world, the principles, the geometry; show me undoubted and striking examples of their influence.'[13]

It could not have been put better. Kepler is close to my conclusions when he denies all truth in houses except for those close to the four angles of the horoscope. And the way in which he demands from Fabricius well-founded proof of the existence of the houses through theory and practical experience is completely scientific. History has not recorded what Fabricius replied to Kepler in his own defence.

Kepler is not content just to criticize, however. He puts forward new ideas, for example, the remarkable notion of *astral heredity*, which he was the first to clearly formulate. In Chapter X of his book *DeStella Nova* (On the New Star), he 'wishes to establish that the astral configurations are in analogous positions at the births of children and their parents. [He asserts] that he has observed this

Second Interlude: Kepler: Astronomer, Astrologer

astral heredity in many examples, including his own, which proves how sensitive the soul of man is to configurations which it cannot directly perceive.'[14]

Which mechanism does Kepler propose to account for this *astral atavism*? The retention of celestial information. As a result of the astral configurations at birth, the 'vital faculties' of man undergo a real programming, whose traces will be imprinted in him and produce later effects. Simon asserts:

> At the end of a pregnancy, the vital faculty of the mother is prompted to trigger off labour when the configurations which are forming resemble those imprinted in her at her own birth, or even (because of the attraction of similar persons) of the father's. This is why the child's birth chart often shows so many analogies with those of its parents, and it is profitable to deepen the analysis of a horoscope with the help of this astral heredity.[15]

This is a fundamental notion for Kepler, who also states in *Harmonices Mundi*: 'There is one perfectly clear argument beyond all others in favour of the authenticity of astrology: this is the common horoscopic relation between parents and children.'[16]

This is all very admirable. The way in which Kepler explains astral heredity through the 'triggering off' of birth by an astral configuration, clearly foreshadows the hypothesis I put forward to account for my observations on the *planetary heredity effect*: I spoke of the 'midwife planets'.[17] I shall return to this point later.

Despite all this, my observations do not provide factual confirmation of Kepler's intuition. While delving into this great astronomer's thoughts, one finds a great distance separating his 'romantic', almost religious notion and the astral atavism of the phenomena I have put forward. In a letter to his master, Maestlin, in 1598, he writes:

> These are then the relationships of birth. You have a Sun–Mercury conjunction, so has your son; you both have Mercury after the Sun. You have almost a trine from Saturn to the Moon, he has almost a Moon–Saturn sextile. You have almost a Saturn–Sun trine; and so does he. In place of your Saturn, he has the Sun and Mercury. His and your Venus are in opposition.[18]

This text shows that Kepler believes in the existence of family similarity in *planetary aspects*. I tested Kepler's statement. I compared birthcharts – some 10,000 pairs – of parents and their children. The results, recently published in my book *Planetary Heredity*,[19] are negative. Kepler's alleged similarities do not exist.

Nevertheless, his merit remains. Had I not been acquainted with his idea through my reading of Paul Choisnard's work, I would not have been tempted to study the possibility of planetary heredity – within the strict framework of my results on occupations and traits of character – and to observe a balance of results favourable to this hypothesis. But I shall say more about Choisnard and planetary heredity later.

The idea of astral heredity is all the more interesting for allowing Kepler to short-circuit an objection to astrology which has returned as a leitmotiv since antiquity: Why attach importance to the horoscope of *birth*? It is the horoscope of *conception* that should count.

This objection was already formulated against Ptolemy, who tried to bypass it. Let us follow the subtle reasoning he sets out in *Tetrabiblos*. He first acknowledges the importance of the moment of conception 'for the seed is given once and for all'. However, he goes on to say:

> If [we] do not know the time of conception, which is usually the case, we must follow the starting point furnished by the moment of birth and give to this our attention, for it too is of great importance ... For the child at birth and his bodily form take on many additional attributes which he did not have before, when he was in the womb, those very ones indeed which belong to human nature alone; and even if it seems that the ambient at the time of birth contributes nothing toward his quality, at least his very coming forth into the light under the appropriate conformation of the heavens contributes, since nature, after the child is perfectly formed, gives the impulse to its birth under a configuration of similar type to that which governed the child's formation in detail in the first place (that is, at its conception).[20]

This is slightly complicated, but not badly devised. Robbins, the editor of the English translation of *Tetrabiblos*, is no doubt right to state that here we have an 'assumption which Ptolemy does not think necessary to demonstrate'. But wishing is not enough, you have to know how as well. To verify this postulate, we need to compare the charts of conception to the corresponding birthcharts and observe the astral similarities between them. We are still unable to undertake such a project today as we do not know the exact moment of conception.

Be that as it may, I wanted to dwell on the notion of astral heredity, since it illustrates how astrology – like astronomy – could produce over the centuries legitimate explanatory hypotheses that were cleverly conceived. In the case of Ptolemy and Kepler, of course, the proof was cruelly lacking. The latter showed the utmost courage in endeavouring to understand the mechanism of astral influences; the same courage and same fervour as he put to the service of astronomy. For him, it was the same fight, constantly challenged, for, as Kepler states: 'Our speculations have not exhausted all the treasures of nature, nor have they scientifically established how many senses exist.'[21]

ACT FOUR

The Renaissance

8

THE LAST MAGICIANS

Since antiquity, astrology has had its opponents. The most famous are the Greek, Carneades (*c.* 214–129 B.C.), who founded the New Academy in Athens, and above all, the Roman Cicero (106–43 B.C.), who took up cudgels against it in his book *De Divinatione*: 'If astrology were true, all the soldiers who died in the battle of Cannes would have had to be born on the same day, under the same horoscope!' This seems to me a rather doubtful argument. The Renaissance produced more subtle criticism. In fact, the opponents of astrology did not dispute the possible existence of an astrological *science*. It was against *divinatory* astrology that they rebelled, in the name of nascent humanism and human dignity.

St Thomas Aquinas (1225–74), a believer in astrology, suggested that the planets were guided by Angels who themselves received orders from God. God was, then, the cause of astral influences. With this distinction, Aquinas did much to improve the still unclear relations between astrologers and Church dignitaries. The well-known adage that ensued, *Astra inclinant non necessitant* (the stars give tendencies, not imperatives), did much to calm spirits. In any case, many astrologers used it as an alibi, through either cunning or conviction. Not all did, though.

In 1362, the plague raged in Padua and the astrologers, as always in troubled times, tried to explain this earthly catastrophe through particularly unfavourable celestial aspects. Petrarch (1304–74), the famous Italian poet, challenged this:

> Leave free the paths of truth and of life ... These globes of fire cannot be guides for us ... The virtuous souls, stretching forward to

their sublime destiny, shine with a more beautiful inner light. Illuminated by these rays, we have no need of these swindling astrologers and lying prophets who empty the coffers of their credulous followers of gold, who deafen their ears with nonsense, corrupt judgment with their errors, and disturb our present life and make people sad with false fears of the future.[1]

Notwithstanding this vigorous denunciation, Petrarch had a perfect knowledge of the astrological gods. 'In one of his poems,' states Seznec, 'Petrarch describes in 123 verses the visual details indicative of the pose, costume, and attributes of each god.' The classic opposition in astrology between Jupiter and Saturn was known to him: 'First Jupiter, superb on his majestic seat, holding in hand his sceptre and thunderbolt . . . then, with heavy pace and saddened by old age, with veil on hand and clothed in greyish cloak, came Saturn, holding in his hand – like a peasant – a rake and a sickle.'[2]

But more than a poet was needed to seriously weaken astrology. The attack needed to be scientific. It was conducted, more than a century later, by Pico della Mirandola, a man of brilliance – some even say genius – who died young (1463–94), allegedly poisoned by his secretary. Nevertheless, Pico had time to publish his famous work *Disputationes*, which was to arouse much controversy and exert an enduring influence on astrologers. In response to his criticisms, they tried to do better.

Pico's arguments were very modern, and they remain of interest today in the context of a revolution of the foundations of astrology. In his book *The Occult Sciences in the Renaissance*, Wayne Shumaker writes about Pico:

> The principle which underlies most of his denials is that the planets act upon human beings only by light and motion and have no more secret influences at all . . . Further, the light, together with the heat which it contains . . . acts universally and cannot be held responsible for individual differences in human beings. For the time, these insights were exceptional.[3]

Indeed, these same reasons for rejecting astrology have been taken up by contemporary astronomers. Pico also asserts:

The Last Magicians

> An event in the distant future cannot be caused by a present configuration. Astrologers predict the influence on the early part of life of a planet which lies in the east, and on the late years of a planet which lies in the west; and so on, through many refinements. This, however, is to say that a heavenly force is more powerful when it does not exist than when it does. Forces which are to produce something in the future also produce it more powerfully in the present.[4]

Pico returns to this subject in Book X of *Disputationes* by taking, more specifically, the doctrine of houses as his target. Shumaker comments: 'In space itself Pico will admit no significance beyond that of determining the angle at which rays impinge upon us. Empty areas of the sky possess no inherent "virtue". This is imputed to them, however, by the doctrine of houses, which he proceeds to criticize in detail.'[5]

Pico goes on at length about the arbitrariness of the significance of houses, as being due merely to doubtful analogies, stating:

> The father loves his sons, and the fifth house is connected with the Ascendant by a trigonal, hence friendly angle; therefore the fifth house signifies sons ... The first house is that of the nativity because *de tenebris prodit in lucem*, from darkness it comes forth into light ... Similarly, the second house has to do with riches because, they say, nothing is nearer to a man than riches, and the second house adjoins the first [etc.].[6]

Pico is, of course, right in rejecting the arbitrariness of the twelve houses, but he goes too far in his criticism of astral influences, for he refuses, on the same grounds of 'absurdity', to believe that the Moon influences the tides. He states: 'Nothing forces us to admit that there is a new power in the Moon, other than movement and light, through which it moves the sea.'[7] This 'new power' of the Moon is simply gravitation, which would be discovered later. As for the notion of 'absurdity', in science it is a relative notion.

Disputationes has remained a classic, but it did not succeed in stopping the development of astrology in the Renaissance, nor its application to, for example, medicine.

*

Neo-Astrology

Paracelsus (1493–1541), the father of hermetic medicine, was at the same time a practitioner and a theoretician of science and astrological philosophy. But above all, Paracelsus was a doctor and his aim was to cure the sick. For him, the microcosm–macrocosm doctrine was not simply to remain an attractive theory but it opened up the way to effective cures. This fiery theoretician believed in a correspondence between the external world, particularly the heavens, and the different parts of the internal world, the human organism. He thought that a doctor should always consult the stars before writing a prescription.

'For Paracelsus,' writes Guy Bechtel, 'a medicine is founded on four pillars: philosophy, astronomy, alchemy and a last notion, more difficult to grasp, which he calls *proprietas*, a Latin word that may be translated here as virtue.'[8] Philosophy is in harmony with the doctrine of correspondence between the microcosm and the macrocosm: 'It is only through knowledge of natural philosophy, that is, of the relation between the worlds and beings, that we can find the way to cures. We must see man through the whole universe.'[9] Bechtel goes on:

> Astronomy naturally plays a vital role. We can only understand man through the heavens, because we are the sons of the heavens. Everything is interwoven and, to heal, we must return to the origin of the illness. This, in fact, does not come from man ... A doctor then, Paracelsus says, *needs to be astral*. The study of the external heavens teaches him about the internal heavens and indicates the origin of the corruption which occurred and revealed itself as an illness. He learns about the interior through the exterior ... There is a time to be ill and a time to cure. Remedies cannot in fact be effective if they are in opposition to astral properties.[10]

In the therapeutic and practical field, a few quotes from Paracelsus will suffice to judge how he perceived the role of doctor. In his book *Paragranum* (1530), he describes the four pillars of medicine, starting with philosophy:

> [As man] is at the same time the heaven and the earth ... the path of the philosopher is therefore twofold ... a similar division is

> relevant to the four elements. Heaven and earth are separated, just as there are two arms, two legs, two eyes, the upper and lower jaw; like the flesh of the feet and that of the cheek. To a fiery celestial Saturn corresponds a terrestrial Saturn. There is an aquatic Sun and a celestial Sun ... What is the terrestrial Venus if not the womb, hidden in the stomach? The terrestrial Venus teaches the doctor about the womb. Human conception has Venus of the world as its agent. The spermatic vessels will remain empty if the vessels of Venus are not favourable. Iron is nothing without Mars. Mars is iron, and vice versa. For man, there is no difference between the Suns, Moons, Mercurys, Saturns, Jupiters except that which determines their aspects.[11]

'As above so below,' declared the legendary Hermes Trismegistus, and Paracelsus completely supported this new conception of the world.

But let us look at the other basis for medicine, which is, according to Paracelsus, astronomy. This is what interests us here the most:

> What I said of philosophy, especially applies to astronomy ... There is, within and without man, a heaven, and air; just as the bodily balm corresponds to the terrestrial balm, the Milky Way is within us ... It may appear strange to you, humoralist physicians, that the galaxy crosses the stomach, that there are within man two poles, planets, and a zodiac. You also thought it strange that balm grows in the stomach and iron rusts inside the body ... To cure a man, the doctor must understand the heavens within man ... Moreover, note that the heavens react within us. Therefore, how can we identify this action if we do not have knowledge of the celestial properties? ... only he who judges of the interior heavens is a physician. If his only knowledge is of the external heavens, he remains an astronomer and astrologer, but if he achieves in himself an equilibrium between these two sciences, he will know two heavens. [This physician, this wise man] must know in each man, in the crowd and actuality of types, the state of the heavens and of their harmony, in order to have an understanding of health, sickness, the beginning, the term, the end, death, for the heavens are man, and vice versa. All men are one heaven and the heaven is but a single man.[12]

Nevertheless, Paracelsus knew how unequally the fate and health of beings on earth were shared out from the moment of birth:

> If the heavens were single and there was only one celestial movement, there would be only one man and one heaven; and all men would be ill and recover their health at the same time. But there is no such thing as absolute uniformity. Uniformity is broken at the moment of celestial birth. At the time of its conception the child inherits, in effect, a particular heaven. If all children were born in the same place, there would only be one heaven, one celestial movement. The great heaven influences the heaven at birth in a marvellous way. One might, in fact, think that it is impossible – since ten thousand children are born each day – that each should have its own heaven, as different one from any other heaven as East and West ... Just as a tree, starting from a seed, sprouts and develops, spreading and growing from the earth, the hours become longer from the earth to the sky. Just as the tree is much larger than the seed, the astral hour is much longer than the earthly hour, and earthly minutes correspond in the sky to whole months.[13]

Although Paracelsus sometimes becomes repetitive in his desire to convince, I have quoted him here not only because of his considerable influence on medicine but also because he perfectly illustrates Renaissance ideas on the subject of astrology. Astrology was everywhere: just as Kepler was an astronomer-astrologer, Paracelsus was a physician-astrologer.

The Renaissance also produced a large number of *pure* astrologers. Some became rich and famous working for men in high places, others were more obscure and remained impecunious. There were also 'researchers', who, bearing in mind Pico's criticism, tried – sometimes clumsily – to improve on the doctrine of astral influences. I have chosen to mention three who, on several accounts, are of particular interest for my purpose: Morin, Bonatti and Placidus. It should be stressed that these three authors were published at the very end of the Renaissance period, when, ironically, the astrological star was about to suffer a new and prolonged eclipse in the scholarly circles of the European intelligentsia.

Jean-Baptiste Morin of Villefranche, who worked during the first part of the seventeenth century, was the last 'official' astrologer of the French court. He cast the horoscope of the Dauphin, the future

The Last Magicians

'Sun-King', Louis XIV. Right after his death, his *Astrologica Gallica* was published, a lengthy astrological treatise in several volumes (1661). Shumaker writes that this work 'was highly regarded by Jean Hiéroz, a vigorous modern propagandist, who saw in the work "rather the earliest treatment of scientific astrology than the last of traditional astrology".'[14] He however considers, and I share his opinion, that Morin was only an 'advanced traditionalist'.

Morin interests me most as the author of another work, *La théorie des déterminations astrologiques* (The Theory of Astrological Determinations), in which he explains the influence of planets on the various professions. As I summarized in Table 1 (see p. 25) the basis of my observations in favour of astral influence is found in the planet-occupation correlation. I was therefore curious to compare Morin's claims and my results. Here, according to Morin, are the professions towards which the planets give an impulse when they are in a 'a good celestial state':

Saturn: men of science and learning; theologians, philosophers, mathematicians, treasurers, sculptors, architects, mining engineers;
Jupiter: men of government, statesmen, governors of provinces, counsellors, presidents, chancellors, diplomats, politicians; magistrates, prefects, mayors. High dignitaries of the Church; dignitaries of the Court;
Mars: men of war, hunters, lawyers, doctors, blacksmiths;
Sun: popes, emperors, kings, princes, governors, magnates, noblemen, all those on to whom honours and dignity are conferred, ambassadors;
Venus: artists, musicians, members of the holy orders, pharmacists, perfumers, weavers, jewellers;
Mercury: arithmeticians, geometers, astrologers, astronomers, philosophers, orators, writers, poets, painters, scribes, secretaries, negotiators, inventors, skilled craftsmen;
Moon: queens, princesses, widows, travellers, fishermen, hunters, the people.[15]

I have not yet worked on all the occupations mentioned by Morin. Some are surprising: 'widows' or 'nobles' are for example states which do not appear to be professional activities as such. But we cannot judge Morin fairly without taking into account the evolution of moral standards since the time of Louis XIV. Some occupations have disappeared, and others taken their place.

With reference to Table 1 (see p. 25) I can nevertheless draw a comparison. Among those occupations that agree with the professional groups defined, I note for Saturn: men of science and learning, mathematicians; for Jupiter: men of government, statesmen, presidents, chancellors, politicians, high dignitaries; for Venus (but this remains to be proved more firmly through further research): artists, musicians; and lastly, I willingly grant that the relationship established by Morin between the Moon and 'the people' reflects a certain truth: I have observed that politicians tended to be born when the Moon was in the Gauquelin sectors.

Among those occupations that do not agree with my findings generally I will single out, for Saturn: philosophers (born under the Moon, according to my results), and sculptors to whose birth I have not been able to link a particular planet; for Jupiter: bishops, who are not usually born under this planet (though it may be noted that bishops of the *ancien régime* were as much servants of the State as of the Church, unlike the 'republican' bishops whose birth data I have collected), and, above all, men of war and actors, who are not included. A more serious disagreement is that Morin does not attribute the Moon to writers and poets (who are, in fact, mostly born under this planet), assigning them instead to Mercury. Moreover, he wrongly associates Mercury with geometers, astronomers (born, according to my findings under Saturn), or painters. It is difficult to establish whether the occupations on which Morin and myself agree outweigh those on which we don't. It must be pointed out, however, that by planets in 'a good celestial state', Morin never meant that the planets were positioned after the horizon or meridian – i.e. in the Gauquelin zones – but instead referred to, and I quote: 'the position of the planet in a *zodiacal sign* and to the quality of its aspects', which is not at all the same thing. Even so, the chances that Morin's and my own findings would be in agreement were, at the outset so slight that the fact that they are is in itself quite remarkable in the field of planetary symbolism. (I will return to this point later.) One thing is nevertheless certain: Morin, like his colleagues since Ptolemy, claims that there are 'occupational' (professional) planets, and in this, if my work is valid, he is actually correct.

The fact still remains that Morin, as Shumaker rightly comments, 'neither attacks nor defends astrology at its roots, where it is at its most vulnerable'. It seems that he did not know, or did not want to answer, Pico's objections. To quote Shumaker again: 'What appears to have been the latest work within the limits of our period to attempt this was the *Universa Astrosophia Naturalis* of Antonio Francesco de Bonatti published in 1687.' In the *same year*, by a historical quirk, *Principia*, Newton's fundamental work on gravity, was published. Shumaker goes on:

> Bonatti, who was very earnest, intended to make his case for astrology by reason and authority in Book I and by *experientia* in Book II. He had studied the subject from early youth but found it obscured by so many errors and superstitions that hardly any ray of truth appeared in it. In the end, however, he decided that notwithstanding inaccurate comprehension of many causes and effects and of some of the heavenly motions, 'something probably truthful and scientific could always be discerned'. He has accordingly ... like the cultivator who carefully roots poisonous plants out of his stubborn fields lest the fruitful ones be spoiled. To be sure, the establishment of probable judgements requires from 200 to 300 years of observation; but we have accurate observations from former centuries, annotated and digested into tables, and he has used these in giving examples of accurate predictions about death. For the rest, he has treated astrology as a natural science which raises the mind to contemplation of God.[16]

Bonatti thought as a physicist, not as an occultist. He believed that the astral influences depended only on the *real* positions and that the radiance of the celestial bodies reached its maximum intensity when the planets were culminating. An important part of his work, as Shumaker points out, was a purely experimental endeavour:

> We ... must look briefly at his 329 pages of horoscopes, which are intended as experimental justification of astrological truths. This

second part of his book comes nearer than anything else I have found to anticipating the attempts of Choisnard, Jung, and other modern investigators to offer an authentically inductive verification.[17]

Bonatti's results strengthened his conviction that the world of men was connected to the stars because the upper world was linked to the lower one, macrocosm to microcosm.

In a way, he was to the end of the Renaissance period, what Vettius Valens had been to the flourishing Roman Empire. The idea of collecting numerous cases is a very 'statistical' one. Bonatti went further than Vettius Valens in *quantity* – Valens worked on 138 cases, Bonnatti on 329 – but above all in *quality*:

> The horoscopes are grouped in sections which have to do with persons who died in infancy or early childhood, persons who died violently by the sword, fire, water, or falls, persons who met hazards but were still alive, and, finally, some sets of twins. The times of birth, we are told, have been accepted only from public registers (*a mortorum matriculis*) or from trustworthy friends, and all can easily be checked. The results are interesting and impress some readers ... the safeguards were unusual for the period, and of all the defenses of astrology written during the Renaissance, none may come so near to shaking a modern sceptic.[18]

Despite all his efforts, however, Bonatti was unable to convince 'a modern sceptic', or even an 'open-minded modern sceptic'. The evidence he provided remained unreliable (probability calculus did not exist in his time), and he did not have the opportunity to ask the right questions. Nevertheless, I recognize in him, with his careful gathering of birth data, a real precursor.

Bonatti tried to 'purify' and 'prove' astrology through *experiment*. Kepler chose another path: to revolutionize astrology and make it a science equal to astronomy through *mathematical theory*. Neither of them accomplished his Copernican revolution, but this was too soon to come.

Astrology progressed during the Renaissance as a result of the greater accuracy of the astronomical aids which were put to the service of horoscopes. On a limited point of calculus, but one fundamental for contemporary astrologers (and for myself), posterity owes much to an author only a dozen years older than Bonatti, the monk, Placido de Titi.

Placido de Titi, or Placidus de Titis, was born in Perugia (in Ombria, Italy) in 1603. Coming from the noble line of Titi, he was the best representative of Italian neo-scholastic astrology. In his *Histoire de l'astrologie*, Wilhelm Knappich briefly describes the life and work of Placidus:

> At twenty-one, he entered the order of the Olivetans, a Benedictine community which had a house in Sienna. He then became a reader in mathematics and physics in Padua and finally professor at the University of Pavia, where he taught from 1657 until his death in 1668. As is common in monasteries, his followers called him by his Christian name and this is why his system became known as the 'Placidean system' ... [His major work, *Physiomathematica*, shows] how much he was affected by Pico's arguments ... He also tried to prove that all the factors used in astrology are *physical realities* which ensue from natural principles ... The physical reality always came before mathematical concepts.[19]

Placidus's greatest contribution is a method of 'natural' division of houses. 'Because it is here,' he wrote in *Physiomathematica*, 'that all the difference lies between my doctrine and the doctrine of other authors who divide the quantity and space of the sky, while I divide the movement of the stars, and in no way the quantity.' By this, Placidus meant that when the sky is divided into houses, their limits should not be determined by circles of position, as taught by Campanus and Regiomontanus before him, but by adopting a natural astronomical process, 'a proportional division of daily and nightly arcs, each division corresponding to two hours in time.'

In 1657, Placidus published his *Tables of the* Primum Mobile – that is tables of houses – accompanied by thirty examples of birth data. These deserve some attention. They were highly successful when they were published and were reprinted several times. Placidus's system of dividing houses still remains today the one most commonly used by astrologers – although Heaven knows that the competition between the various systems is fierce! The renown of the Placidean tables is also due to luck: frequent reprints have made them accessible to all those who, at the dawn of the twentieth century, were developing an interest in astrology for the first time. The tables were there, and available: they were frequently used without any knowledge of astronomy, or of the mathematical reasons justifying the Placidean division.

I should like here to digress and pay my dues, so to speak, to Placidus. When, as a very young man, I began casting horoscopes, I came across the Placidean tables of houses in the appendix of a very popular astrological book by someone called Maurice Privat. They were completely anonymous tables that Privat, more a journalist than an astrologer, had discovered in a book by another author. I later found out they were the Placidean tables of houses and soon learnt that there were other tables, based on other methods, and more popular with some.

At the time I knew nothing of the mathematical principles involved in the calculation of the twelve houses and I used the tables which were at hand, without giving much thought to the astronomical realities. It was only when, a few years later, I acquired on the quay of the Seine a second-hand copy of *La domification*,[20] by Henri Selva (first published in 1917), that I really understood Placidus and realized the superiority of his system of houses compared with others.

I use the word 'superiority' here only from an astronomical point of view. Placidus – referring to Ptolemy – used it himself; his system is the only one which offers a proportional division of diurnal and nocturnal arcs. All six diurnal houses last for the same amount of time as the diurnal movement – and the same applies to the six nocturnal houses – following the rotation of the Earth on its axis in twenty-four hours. Placidus's is the only valid procedure if one is carrying out statistical research.

Admittedly, I departed from his system when it occurred to me that there was no good reason to retain the division into twelve houses, and that, by using the Placidean method, eighteen, thirty-six, or even more 'houses' could be calculated for each birth. When

The Last Magicians

I first started on my work, I began by dividing each of Placidus's houses into three equal parts, thus avoiding the trouble of calculating the limits of the intermediate sections, which caused some imprecision of no great consequence.

From there, I brought in two innovations. Firstly the term 'houses' seemed to me outdated, so I gave my thirty-six 'houses' a more modern name: 'sectors'. Secondly I numbered them in the direction of the diurnal movement, that is, clockwise. I then compiled my first statistics on the birth data of the members of the Académie de Médecine (see p. 23). My tables imply a very different conception of the various zones of the sky, and this leads me to the third innovation: the division into thirty-six sectors was for me only a practical procedure, to aid my statistical work. The thirty-six sectors were all like the thirty-six numbers of the roulette wheel in casinos (excepting the zero) a priori of equal value; there was no astrological significance attached to them. In this too I moved away from Placidus and his system of traditional houses.

I still have those 'tables', written in my own hand in 1951, in a notebook of squared paper with a green cover. For clarity, I have used two different ink colours, red and blue, and to this day the cover, on which I clumsily spilt a bottle of red ink, looks bloodstained: a moving testimony of my first neo-astrological crime.

Soon, I decided that the thirty-six sector limits should be calculated, and to that effect, I followed a method that was rather complicated but clearly explained in Selva's book. The work was completed by my former wife, Françoise, and we published the tables in *Méthodes* (1957).[21] Today, it is only of a historical value. There are now computer programs that allow very fast and much better calculation of the thirty-six Gauquelin sectors. The method used is even more satisfactory: the diurnal and nocturnal arcs are divided into equal sectors, based on the amount of time that elapses between the rising and setting of a planet (for more details, I refer the reader to the appendix of my work, *Written in the Stars*).[22]

Thus I do owe something to both Bonatti and Placidus. To the former, for his care in collecting birth data. (In the beginning, I did no better than him, lacking experience and method at the age of twenty.) To the latter, for the tables of houses. (End of the disgression!)

Morin, Bonatti and Placidus published their works in the second half of the seventeenth century, as the Renaissance was ending. Astrology had begun to lose its influence among intellectuals. After Kepler's, Bonatti's work represents the last effort to define astrology as a natural science and not simply as a philosophical doctrine – an effort which remained in vain, as it was rejected by men of science: in 1660, by the Royal Society; in 1666 by the Académie des Sciences. It is now more than three centuries since astrology, excluded from the university, has ceased to be an 'official' science.

Nevertheless, it is clear that astrology, equal to medicine for Paracelsus, and to astronomy for Kepler, has been defended by great minds who have tried to revise it and whose insights deserve to be taken up again and studied thoroughly. With the arrival of the encyclopaedists Diderot and d'Alembert, and with the sarcasm of Voltaire, a leaden weight suppressed any serious attempt to restore astrology to the paramount place it had previously occupied. During the Age of Enlightenment there was a total lack of interest in it, and it survived only in its popular form, through almanacs. Newton published his work on the universal law of gravity, and knowledge of the mechanism of the universe advanced in giant strides, abandoning astrology on its way.

Sir Isaac Newton (1642–1727) has long been considered the prototype of the 'modern' scientist, a mind freed from all traces of the occult; it has also been long maintained (especially in scientific circles) that the law of gravity, even more than Copernicus's work, was the death knell of astrology. In the last few years, this attitude has changed, thanks to a greater understanding of Newton and of his 'bizarre' intellectual enquiries; thanks also to a better perception of what astrology really represents.

Who then was Sir Isaac Newton? 'Lord Keynes,' writes Thorndike, 'in a brilliant contribution to the Newton tercentenary celebration (1947) takes the words out of my mouth ... by representing the supreme figure of the experimental science of the seventeenth century as "the last of the magicians", and "the last wonder-child to whom the Magi could do sincere and appropriate homage".'[23] We now know that Newton spent more time studying theology and biblical chronology than writing *Principia* (1687). in which he sets out his theory of gravity. Even better: it has been counted that he devoted 650,000 words to alchemy in the manuscripts which were found at his home. What are we to make of this? Did the author of gravitation theory take Hermes Trismegistus, that mysterious mythical figure, seriously? Probably.

'Many of those – maybe even most of them – who caused revolutionary changes in the knowledge of nature (such as Paracelsus, Cardan, Copernicus, Bruno, Kepler, to cite the most important ones) were motivated by a profound belief that occult forces operate beyond our immediate sensation,' states another science historian, W. Wightman.[24] Pierre Thuillier goes further:

> The facts are clear. Newton copied out numerous texts which were concerned not only with the technical aspects of the 'great art' (alchemy), but also, for example, with the alchemical significance of pagan mythology. Over and above this, there are good reasons to believe that he accepted the existence of an alchemical revelation, in the noble and profound sense of the word. [For Newton] nature represents a sort of great still in which fluids and spirits perpetually circulate ... For example, to explain why certain fluids do not mix, he evokes a 'secret principle of unsociability'. Conversely, the 'vital ether spirit' can be 'sociable' in regard to the marrow and vital juices. He rediscovers the great alchemical theme of secret *sympathies* and *antipathies* which reign among all things. This language is, in a way, close to 'magic'.[25]

Newton may also have devoted some time to astrology. Some astrologers have asserted this on several occasions, quoting one of his letters, but it is now known that the text refers to alchemy and not astrology. It is to be regretted that Newton did not become interested in astrology, as he was in astronomy: he might have advanced by three centuries the theory of astral influences.

For – to take this idea a little further – the fundamental question which Newton dealt with in *astronomy* is close to what Ptolemy and Kepler had earlier asked themselves in *astrology*. For Kepler, the

Neo-Astrology

problem was: how do the stars 'act from a distance' on man? For Newton, the problem was: how can we understand the force of attraction exerted between two objects? To quote Thuillier again:

> The mechanistic Descartes had the vortex of fine matter to provide an intelligible explanation ... But although Descartes proposed *causes* which are easily imagined, he did little to advance dynamics as a quantitative science. We can agree, with R. S. Westfall, that mechanistic philosophy led to a few dead-ends as soon as it dealt with the study of forces. What is remarkable is that Newton, relying on ideas of a quite different origin, was able to go further. In particular, by sublimating animism and natural magic, as we have mentioned, he developed a very comprehensive and effective concept of *force*. Henceforth, it was no longer necessary to refer only to the impact between objects, the impetus through contact: *attraction from a distance* was becoming a scientifically legitimate force. It is appropriate here to assess this innovation at its true value, to discover why it was difficult to formulate. How to think of, how to conceive the way in which the 'attractive force' worked? Should one attribute to each object a little *soul*, a sort of *will*, capable of setting off and maintaining movement towards another object? Was it scientifically reasonable to accept a sort of telepathy which acted without any material support? Also, Newton's theory of attraction was sharply criticized. The supporters of mechanism saw in this a return to the *occult forces* they had been trying so hard to be rid of.[26]

Had he lived in Newton's time, Pico would not have failed to criticize this notion of action from a distance, just as in his lifetime he criticized astrology and the theory of tides as being incompatible with the laws of physics. For 'Newton's system,' according to Thuillier, 'if only indirectly, was effectively rooted in a dubious hermetic tradition.'[27]

At the beginning of this book, I quoted the remark of the science historian, Thorndike, who asserts that the universal law of gravity has replaced another universal law, which is none other than astrology. But, according to him, these two laws are both 'rooted in the same suspect hermetic tradition'. He also writes:

> Mark Graubard has recently written of astrology not as a past superstition but as a fossil science. Yet he does not seem to realize that it depended upon a once generally accepted hypothesis of universal law. . . . [For Roger Bacon, for example] rays of light and of astrological influence were propagated from the same heavenly bodies in accordance with the natural law of the universe, the causation of inferiors by superiors . . . It was quite logical and natural . . . to ask such questions.[28]

There were, however, important areas where the law of gravity did not replace the astrological law: the relation between the mind and the stars; between the body and planetary movement. The astrological law remained intact for everything concerned with biology, medicine and – above all – *psychology*. For science these areas remained 'open fields'. Thus, it was psychological astrology that was to prevail in the Renaissance.

9

SATURN AND MELANCHOLY

The theory of astral 'signatures' was to have a considerable influence on all Renaissance thought. What does 'signature' really mean here? For an explanation of this astral magic, we will turn to Cornelius Agrippa (1486–1535), and his work *De Occulta Philosophia*: 'Agrippa informs us specifically that the body, actions, and dispositions of man are under the influence of one or more of the planets . . . Now each of the planets, having its peculiar nature and property, is possessed of a *seal* or *character* which (through stellar rays) is impressed on inferior things subject to it.'[1]

The seven planetary temperaments became the main themes of astrology. They persuaded the whole of the Renaissance civilization: art, philosophy, science, literature. Of course, the classical horoscope, with its Greek foundations, was still present, but planetary temperaments were the main interest. They became stereotypes that were understood not only by specialists but by all cultured people. The Renaissance intelligentsia thought only in terms of temperaments. By giving a few examples from the abundant Renaissance literature, I hope to show that these stereotypes were a partially correct reflection of reality.

During the Renaissance, the temperament of Saturn was the object of particular interest, and I will therefore take it as an example, and show its development through several famous Renaissance authors. I will then compare the descriptions of its temperament with the results of my statistical enquiries on traits of character in relation to its position at birth. This comparison is, I think, enlightening. In the next chapter, I will deal more briefly with the other planetary temperaments.

Saturn and Melancholy

Everything started – or rather, re-started – with the publication in 1460 of Marsilio Ficino's *Corpus Hermeticum*. This work, in which he revived the ancient Greek hermetic tradition, considerably influenced Renaissance thought. Ficino (1433–99) writes in it about the influence of the planets, and that of Saturn in particular. Jean Seznec described Ficino's attitude to this subject as follows:

> He maintains that the stars, if they do influence the body, have no compulsive power over the soul; but at the same time his own inner life is shadowed by fear of Saturn, the sinister ancient who presided over his birth. He knows that he cannot escape that baleful influence, which condemns him to melancholy. At the most, he can try to turn it into other channels, to use it for good: Saturn, demon of inertia and sterility, is also the presiding genius of intellectual concentration. But even so, Saturn's patronage imposes strict limitations on those to whom it extends, and it is only within these limitations that man is free to shape his personality. This conviction literally obsesses Ficino, and his friends try in vain to distract him from his sombre thoughts.[2]

In his *Epistolae* (Florence, 1495), Ficino complains to his friend, Cavalcanti about the malefic influence of Saturn. Cavalcanti tries to reassure him by telling him it is impossible for the stars to do any harm to man. But Ficino continues to lament. Saturn can, he admits, have a good effect, but 'I am too frightened of its malefic effects'; and then he returns to his own horoscope: 'This melancholy temperament seems to have been imposed on me from the beginning by Saturn, *set almost in the centre of my Ascendant sign*.'[3] (I have emphasized this last part because it indicates that Ficino was born around the time when Saturn was rising, that is, in my terminology, in a zone of strong intensity – see Fig. 2, on p. 27.)

Robert Burton (1577–1640), the famous author of *Anatomy of Melancholy* (1621), is an even more remarkable example of a person born with a dominant Saturn. J. C. Eade writes: 'The horoscope of his own nativity that Robert Burton recorded in his Diary survives to this day.'[4] It is a precious document for the researcher, and I reproduce it here in Figure 8a. It is completely

Neo-Astrology

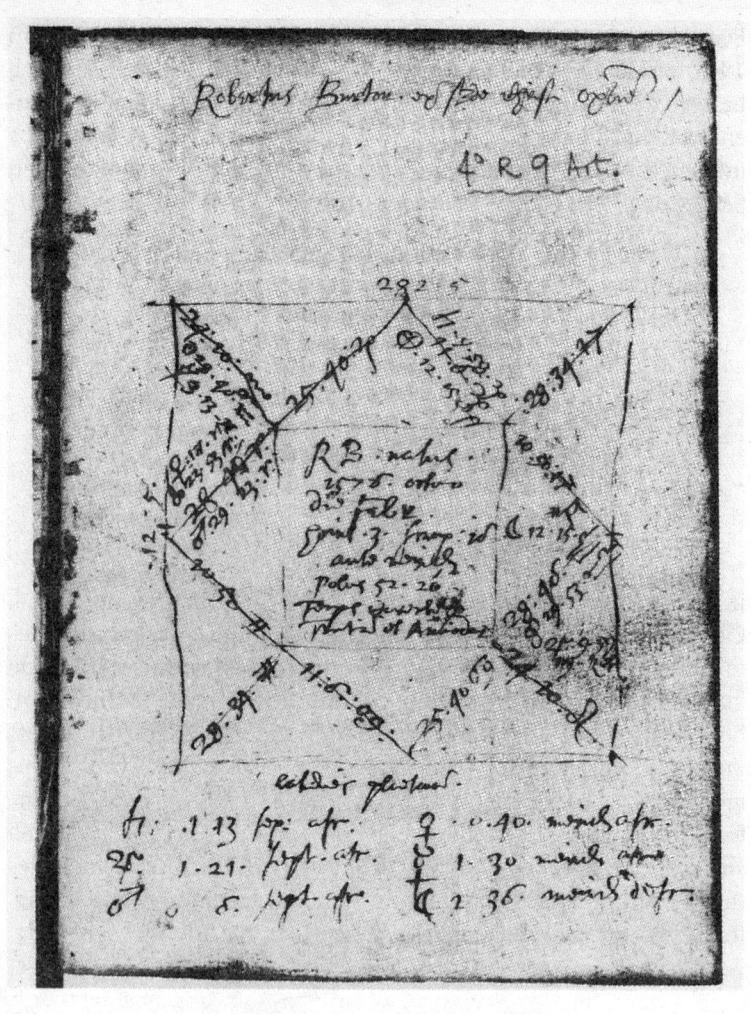

Figure 8a: Robert Burton's horoscope:*
Taken from his diary; note that in the Renaissance the
horoscope was drawn up as a square, not as a circle.
* Born in Lindley, Lincolnshire, on 8 February 1577,
at 8.44 am, latitude 52°20′.

Saturn and Melancholy

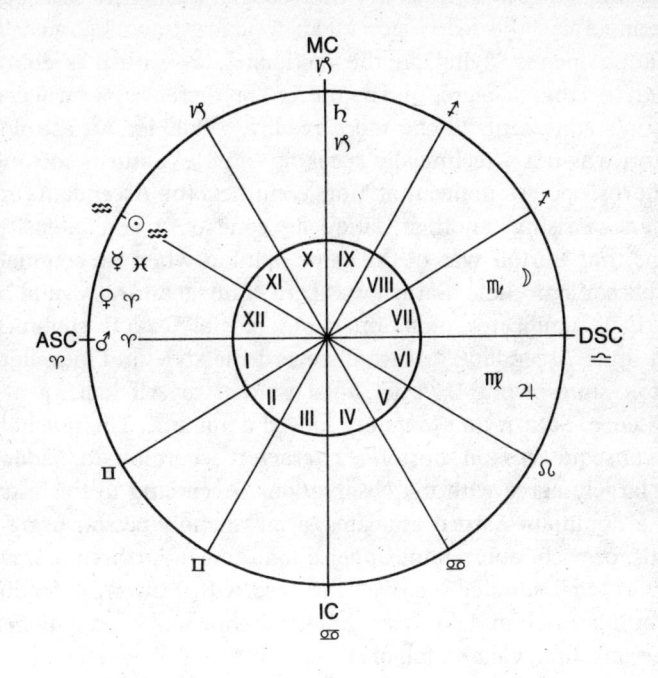

Figure 8b: Robert Burton's horoscope:
A modern graphic representation (based on Figure 8a).

---

clear to Eade that in the case of Burton, Saturn plays a very prominent role. Burton remarks on it himself in his text *Democritus to the Reader*: 'Saturn was Lord of my geniture, *culminating* ...' I have used emphasis here again because it seems very significant that the author of *Anatomy of Melancholy* should have been born when Saturn was in the Gauquelin zone of culmination, as his horoscope confirms (see Figure 8b). In my work, I have often pointed out the relation of the 'melancholy' disposition to a dominant Saturn in the biographies of the cases I examined.

Neo-Astrology

On the subject of Burton's horoscope, the comments of his contemporary, the astrologer Middleton, are unambiguous: 'Culminating means "lying on the meridian", as Saturn is doing to within less than a degree and a quarter . . . [therefore] we will accept Burton's statement all the more readily.'[5] But, for an astrologer, Burton was not – technically speaking – 'pure' Saturn. Looking at his horoscope, we notice that Mars conjuncts the Ascendant, in the process of rising: another Gauquelin zone of strong intensity. It seems that Burton was of the same opinion when he commented on this configuration: 'Saturn was Lord of my geniture . . . and Mars principal significator of manners, in partial [exact] conjunction with mine Ascendant.'[6] If we disregard the style and formulation, Burton states what I would have written myself looking at his horoscope. Saturn and Mars are indeed dominant. The psychological consequences on Burton's character according to Middleton also largely agree with my observations. According to this astrologer, a dominant Saturn indicates 'a melancholy person using few words: peevish, and retains anger a long time'. Furthermore, when Mars is 'well situated', as was the case with Burton, it produces, according to John Lilly, the famous Renaissance practitioner, a 'generous man, valiant, full of courage, irefull, fierce, violent'.[7]

On the subject of Renaissance astrology Shumaker writes:

> Each of the planets possesses a complex of inherent 'virtues' or 'powers', some of which will be alluded to as the discussion proceeds. Something will be implied by adjectives derived from the planetary names 'saturnine', 'jovial', 'mercurial', 'martial'. 'Lunatic' suggests the connection of the Moon with madness as well as with chastity, purity, childbirth, and much else. Mars is associated not only with war but also with anger, ferocity, and an overbearing temperament, much of this being inferred from its redness and the fact that it is so 'hot'. Because Saturn is cold, moves slowly, and rules the heaviest of the metals, lead, it produces a melancholy temperament but is also associated with gravity (a metaphorical extension of 'weight'), profundity and wit. Burton's *Anatomy of Melancholy* was addressed to scholars, who were thought regularly to be saturnine but sometimes, happily, had some admixture of mercurial quantities.'[8]

Saturn and Melancholy

In the Renaissance, the Saturnine temperament kept some pre-eminence over the others, despite – or maybe because of – its bad reputation. In her remarkable study *The Occult Philosophy*, Frances Yates captures how the Renaissance scholars viewed Saturn: on several levels.

Melencolia I is one of the best-known engravings by the famous Albrecht Dürer (1471–1528). Dating from 1514, it is reproduced here in Figure 9. We may admire the artist's skill, but what was his inspiration? Yates explains how the scholarly studies of three authors: Klibansky, Panofsky and Saxl have shown that *Melencolia I* was based on a passage from Agrippa's *De Occulta Philosophia*. The work of these researchers, published in 1964, is simply entitled *Saturn and Melancholy*.[9] Through a learned discussion dealing with the concept of the four 'humours' in the psychology of antiquity and the Middle Ages, and their illustration in the iconography of the Renaissance, an interpretation of *Melencolia I* emerges. It explains this extraordinary portrait, the gloomy face, absorbed in deep meditation and surrounded by a strange assortments of objects. Yates comments:

> According to the Galenic psychology, dominant through the Middle Ages, the four humours or temperaments into which all men could be classified were the sanguine, the choleric, the phlegmatic, and the melancholic. Sanguine people were active, hopeful, successful, outward-looking; they made good rulers and businessmen. Choleric people were irritable, inclined to fighting. Phlegmatic people were tranquil, somewhat lethargic. Melancholy people were sad, poor, unsuccessful, condemned to the most servile and despised occupations. The theory locked man's psychology into the cosmos, for the four humours correspond to four elements and four planets, as follows:
>
> Sanguine – Air – Jupiter
> Choleric – Fire – Mars
> Phlegmatic – Water – Moon
> Melancholy – Earth – Saturn
>
> The theory was bound up with astrology. If Saturn dominated in a horoscope, the person concerned would be inclined to melancholy; if Jupiter, the outlook would be more hopeful, and so on.[10]

Figure 9: *Melencolia I*,
engraved by Albrecht Dürer, 1514.

Saturn and Melancholy

The most unfortunate of the four was Melancholy-Saturn: black hair, a gloomy countenance and livid colouring due to the predominance of the sombre bile of a melancholic complexion. To quote Yates again:

> His typical physical pose, expressive of his sadness and depression, was to rest his head on his hand. Even his 'gifts', or characteristic occupations, were not attractive. He was good at measuring, numbering, counting but what low and earthly occupations were these compared with the splendid gifts of the sanguine Jupiter man, or the grace and loveliness of those born under Venus! ... Dürer's Melencholy has the livid hue, the swarthy complexion, the 'black face' of the type, and she supports her pensive head on her hand in the characteristic pose. She holds compasses for measuring and numbering. Beside her is the purse, for counting money. Around her are tools, such as an artisan might use. Obviously she is a melancholic ... but she seems also to express some more lofty and intellectual type of behaviour. She is not actually doing anything, just sitting and thinking. What do those geometrical forms mean?[11]

Renaissance astrologers have in common a fear of the harmful influence of a badly placed Saturn. In his book on the influence of astrology on Renaissance literature, Johnstone Parr quotes a few interpretations put forward by the leading lights of the era.[12] Alchabitius explains: 'Saturn is evil ... produces and fosters ... men of melancholic complexion. He signifies ... profound silence ... mistrust and suspicion, moving men to complaints and mutterings.' Augier Ferrier asserts that Saturn makes people 'sadde, solitaire, fearful, melancholie, faint-hearted ... rejecting the counsell of others; fearing that all the world doth deceive him; uncivil ... flying the compagny of men unless it be to deceive them.' Cornelius Agrippa writes: 'The gestures and motions of ... Saturn ... are ... beating of the breast or striking of the hand; ... bowing of the knee, and a fixed look downwards, as of one praying.' And lastly, William Lilly, the most famous authority of his time, characterizes Saturn in his *Christian Astrology* (1647) with these words: 'melancholy, sullenness, silence, sorrow, frowning, weeping, and incivility.'

All this is rather depressing. Is the Saturnine type really as negative as that? Let us return to my results on the traits of character observed in famous people born with a dominant Saturn – therefore in the Gauquelin 'plus zones'. In *Your Personality and the Planets*,[13] there is a list of 100 'Saturnian' traits, among which can be found: anxious, cold, effacing, fearful, gauche, hesitant, *melancholic*, mistrustful, morose, pessimistic, preoccupied, reclusive, sad, self-doubting, silent, solitary, taciturn, timid, withdrawn.'

This extract gives an image similar to that of the Renaissance astrologers' Saturn. It even includes the famous trait: 'melancholic'. However, I have deliberately *chosen* from my list, the most 'negative' traits associated with Saturn that I could find. It is possible to carry out an opposite process, which would involve choosing from the list of the same traits, only those showing a 'positive' side of the Saturnine temperament. For example: assiduous, attentive, austere, calm, dignified, discreet, faithful, industrious, ingenious, laborious, modest, orderly, patient, profound, punctual, scrupulous, serious, sober, wise. In her work, Frances Yates has shown that, even for Saturn, people in the Renaissance also found a positive side to describe.

If we study in depth the thought of the great Renaissance authors – who were not preoccupied only with the 'profane' side of the horoscope – we see a very different picture of the Saturn temperament emerging which needs to be interpreted on different levels. Yates shows how the Renaissance conception of the Saturnine temperament could be 'revalued', to use her expression. Going back to Dürer's engraving, she explains:

> There was a line of thought through which Saturn and the melancholy temperament might be 'revalued', raised from being the lowest of the four (temperaments) to become the highest, the humour of great men, great thinkers... To be melancholic was a sign of genius; the 'gifts' of Saturn, the numbering and measuring studies attributed to the melancholic, were to be cultivated as the highest kind of learning which brought man nearest to the divine. This radical change in the attitude to melancholy had results in affecting a change in the direction of men's minds and studies.[14]

This justifies the 'positive' traits of personality that I have often encountered in relation to a dominant Saturn in eminent people. A temperament that allows one to reach the highest level of scientific success, for example. Had not my very first work, in 1955, shown that famous physicians and scientists are born more frequently than common mortals when Saturn is rising or culminating, thus dominating the horoscope?[15]

Through a number of convincing arguments, too long to go into here, Yates has shown that Dürer was well acquainted with Agrippa's work *De Occulta Philosophia*, that he must have read around 1510, since the manuscript was passed around the circles that Dürer mixed in. In this work, Agrippa in fact describes three types of *humor melancholicus*. According to him, there are three capacities of our soul, namely the *imagination*, the *rational* and the *mental*. If the soul passes through these three stages, it progresses – if it succeeds in reaching the last step, the *intellect* – to knowing 'the secrets of divine matters'. So the Saturnine temperament has thus been transfigured.

This remarkable classification immediately explains the enigmatic title of Dürer's engraving: *Melencolia I*. Why I (one)? This engraving must have depicted the first in the series of three stages described by Agrippa: the one relating to the imagination. 'In fact we see in the engraving the tools, the geometric figures, alluding to the traditional "occupation of Saturn", his skills in number and measurement, but transmuted in the atmosphere of inspired melancholy to become the instruments of inspired artistic genius.'[16] If this is the right interpretation, what has happened to 'Melencolia II' and 'Melencolia III'? asks Yates. The engraving that we have does not present us with a complete solution to the problem of inspired melancholy, as Dürer saw it. Yates resolves this enigma by employing ingenius computations. Unfortunately, by mentioning them here, I would wander too far from my subject.

From these conceptions came the legend of the Saturnine type of 'inspired' melancholy. The Elizabethan theatre made great use of it and Shakespeare made obvious allusions. The Melancholy Jaques in

As You Like It (1623) represents inspired melancholy of a moralizing nature. In his retreat 'under the shade of melancholy boughs', in the Forest of Arden 'he watches scenes from the life of man from the cradle to the grave, described in his famous speech. Jaques's insight, his moralizing on the time is akin to folly ... He is the melancholic who is inspired to speak the truth ... Jaques and his Melancholy are in tune with the mourning, weeping, Saturnian, malcontent humour'[17] which I described earlier on. But, continues Yates:

> The Melancholy Jaques is but a preparation for the appearance of the most famous melancholic of all time: Hamlet, Prince of Denmark ... There can be no doubt that Hamlet belongs to Melancholy Night but is it a good melancholy of inspired vision or a bad melancholy of witchcraft and evil? [Whatever he may be,] like the Melancholy Jaques who must 'cleanse the body of the infected world', Hamlet regards the situation with which he has to deal as a 'nasty sty'. Hamlet's black humour is the melancholy of a prophet in a world so badly disobedient to the Law that the universal harmony is inaudible, or broken, like sweet bells jangled out of tune and harsh.[18]

In their book *Born Under Saturn: the Character and Conduct of Artists*, Rudolf and Margot Wittkower show how the notion of the Saturnine artist creating in solitude gained currency in the Renaissance. They state the following in their preface:

> Philosophers discovered that the emancipated artists of their time showed the characteristics of the Saturnine temperament: they were contemplative, meditating, brooding, solitary, creative. At that critical moment in history arose the new image of the alienated artist. Even where he is not mentioned, the sinister ancient god looms large behind many of the following pages ... Many artists of the late fifteenth century and the first half of the sixteenth conform to this type. When they aligned themselves with scholars and poets, they stepped outside the pale and developed symptoms, often to an excessive degree, of the class they joined.[19]

A sort of stereotype was created, which was not without affectation. The Wittkowers point out, through a number of portraits of artists, that many of them in fact did not display this melancholic and

Saturn and Melancholy

Saturnian behaviour, and that, over the centuries, this stereotype has more or less disappeared. A last echo of it is possibly to be found in the bitter declaration of the French poet, Paul Verlaine, when bemoaning his states of mind: *'Tout cela vient de ce que je suis Saturnien!'* (All this is because I am Saturnian). In fact, Verlaine was not born while Saturn was in a strong position, but under the Moon, like many poets.

Since André Murger in the last century wrote *The Bohemian Life* – the novel which was taken by Puccini as the basis for his famous opera – we have discovered that the artist or poet is often the complete antithesis of Saturn: carefree, gregarious, light, extravagant, disorganized. A psychological profile that has in turn become, in our time, a stereotype, even a generally accepted idea.

But can we compare Michelangelo, who suffered all the agonies of seclusion, and the moustache of Salvador Dali? The status of the artist has evolved over the centuries and values are no longer the same. My research on the birth data of artists – painters, musicians, poets, actors – has shown that they have a tendency to 'avoid' being born when Saturn is rising or culminating (see Table 1, on p. 25). They are *less often* Saturnine than the average person. This is not necessarily in contradiction with what the Renaissance scholars thought. In fact, because the time of birth was not written in official civil records before the nineteenth century, or even the twentieth, my sample of artists, of necessity, has been centred on that period when 'the bohemian life' prevailed over solitary creation. My statistical observations agree then with a 'counter-image' of Saturn in the Renaissance.

Starting with the sombre, evil and baleful Saturn of the Greek astrologers, Renaissance scholars gradually 'rehabilitated' the influence of the planet. It is a very original contribution, and one that has been confirmed by surveys of great Saturnian men. No doubt, Saturn always leads to melancholy and solitude (and it remains malefic in popular horoscopes). But withdrawal into oneself is a crucible for the concentration of thought, which then becomes creative.

10

CHILDREN OF THE PLANETS

In the Renaissance, the Saturnine temperament was not dissociated from other planetary 'signatures' whose names are today still those of the pagan gods of antiquity. In *The Survival of the Pagan Gods*, Jean Seznec recounts how these gods crossed the centuries and are still as they were, and equally powerful, despite fifteen centuries of Christianity and ten centuries of Islam, two religions both strictly monotheistic and authoritarian. Nothing has changed. They survived, sometimes under amazing disguises, and they reached the Renaissance with the same attributes: the iconography in Seznec's work provides abundant illustrations of this. The people of the Renaissance believed that they were born under the influence of one of these pagan gods. Of course, they no longer used the irreligious term, 'pagan gods': they simply believed that they were the 'children of the planets'. Seznec writes: 'each planetary divinity presides, so to speak, over an assemblage of persons disposed beneath it in series or groups. These are its "children" whose vocation it has determined. Thus, Mercury presides over an assemblage of painters, writers and merchants.'[1] Equally, there are the children of Mars as they are represented in iconography: 'in fury, mounted in a chariot drawn by two horses, helmeted, whip in hand, and accompanied by a wolf.'[2] The children of Jupiter are often pictured on a throne in a stately pose, holding a sceptre – or a thunderbolt. And, of course, there are 'the children of Saturn who, obedient to the law of their star, meditate gloomily and at length on the secrets of wisdom.'[3]

Shumaker briefly outlines the nature of the diverse influences:

Children of the Planets

> The most powerful good influence was believed to be the Sun's; but it required some tempering by the milder Jupiter or Venus ... Jupiter's influence because it resembled the Sun's but lacked the threat of excessiveness, was perhaps the most favourable of all. Venus in consequence of a softness produced by her moisture, combined her influence favourably with that of the dry, and therefore desiccating Sun, but alone tended to produce sensuality. Mercury was lord, among other things, of learning and eloquence ... The 'qualities' of heat, cold, dryness, and moisture were distributed to all seven planets in pairs. The Sun was hot and dry, the moon cold and moist, Venus hot and moist. Othello's observation, in a fit of jealousy, that Desdemona's hand was hot and moist associated her immediately with Venus and lechery.[4]

However, we need to be more precise about the psychological signatures of each planet. Here are a few quotations (excluding Saturn whom we already know) from Renaissance astrologers, which I have borrowed from the work of Johnstone Parr.[5]

For *Mars* 'That the bloody, ireful, and otherwise malefic planet Mars conduces to war, fire, strife, debate, and quarrelling is attested by all of the astrologers.' Albohazen Haly describes the general nature of Mars thus: 'Mars is a planet ... fiery and violent; he is a destroyer and a conqueror, delighting in slaughter and death, in quarrels, brawls, disputes, contest; he is ... quickly moved to vehement and devastating anger ... He inspires wars and battles.' Abraham Ibn Ezra agrees with him: 'Mars ... prognosticates flames of fire, rebellion, ... disputes, blows ... combat, wrath, insults ... effrontery ... assault, cruelty ... brewers of quarrels.'

For *Jupiter*: John Indagine reports that Jupiter, the 'author of rule', is also the author of 'beauty, richess, honor ... wysedome, knowledge, eloquence, and magnanimitie'. Albohazen Haly adds: 'When Jupiter is the sole lord of the horoscope and posited fortunately, he makes the native ... honourable, virtuous and pure, of fine reputation, just, morally upright, frank and free, gentle of disposition; beloved by people who perform beautiful deeds ... He is truthful in speech, honest in deed, and fortunate in all his activities.' But when it is 'unfortunately' positioned in the horoscope, Jupiter can become somewhat negative. Augier Ferrier remarks that in that case Jupiter, 'will give sometimes foolishness ... pride ... prodigality ... yeeld hym an hypocrite, and in place of honestie, it will make hym dreame of tyranny'.

For *Venus*: Ferrier notes: 'Venus ... in good disposition, maketh the man pleasant, merry, dancing, laughing, content, amiable, gracious, and of good conversation.' While Albohazen Haly asserts: '[In a favourable position] Venus makes singers and charming people, ardent lovers of flowers and elegance ... They have genteel manners ... are given to games and various diversions, to laughter and joyous living, rejoicing in the companionship of friends and in eating and drinking. They are benevolent, tender by nature, soft and gentle voiced.' But Venus can be placed in an unfavourable position. As Ferrier writes: 'If Venus is unfortunate, it maketh the man ... too merry, ... given to voluptuousness.' William Lilly confirms: 'When Venus is ill-dignified [she causes one to be] ... riotous, wholly given to dissipation, ... coveting unlawful beds, adulterous, spending his means in alehouses, taverns, among scandalous and loose people.'

For *Mercury*: Indagine affirms: 'Mercury is the minister and giver of wisdom and eloquence ... rhetoricke, subtile workes, and such like.' While Erra Pater remarks that Mercury makes everyone 'eloquent in his speech, and yet addicted to lying'. And William Lily says of a 'badly placed' Mercury in a horoscope, that it is 'the author of subtlety, tricks, devices ... A troublesome wit, a great liar ... cheating and thieving everywhere.'

For the *Moon*: Ferrier remarks that the Moon produces 'inconstancie, lightness of spirite ... susceptible to change'. And William Lilly writes that Luna makes one 'inclined to flit and shift his habitation; unsteadfast ... a vagabond, idle person ... delighting to live beggarly and carelessly' (all the more so if the Moon is 'unfavourably positioned' in the horoscope).

And, finally for the *Sun*: Ferrier comments that the Sun makes everyone 'mannerly, wise, a lover of nobleness, following glory and honour ... worthy, and of great estimation'. Alchabitius adds: 'The Sun signifies friendliness ... mildness ... oratory, mature counsel, stern judgement, magnificence.' While for Albohazen Haly, the Sun

Children of the Planets

'makes an exalted, honest, liberal, and glorious soul who rejoices in sumptuous apparel but is not given to gluttony.'

Knowledge of these varied planetary influences was not confined to Renaissance astrologers: it was part of an intellectual 'baggage' of all educated people at that time, in Italy, France, Germany, England. For example, Shakespeare was aware of them. Several characters in his plays are governed by well-defined planets. To quote Parr:[6]

> Shakespeare is always consistent in assigning the planet which would endow the appropriate qualities. Posthumus was born under the benevolent planet Jupiter, and consequently has a favourable destiny at the end of the play *Cymbeline*. Elizabeth, who weeps throughout Richard III, is indeed 'governed by the *watery* moon' (*Richard III*). Monsieur Parolles would be born under Mars because he would be known as a soldier (*All's Well*):
>
> HELENA Monsieur Parolles, you were born under a charitable star.
> PAROLLES Under Mars I.
> HELENA I especially think, under Mars.
> PAROLLES Why under Mars?
> HELENA The wars hath so kept you under that you must needs be born under Mars.
> PAROLLES When he was predominant.
> HELENA When he was retrograde, I think rather.
> PAROLLES Why think you so?
> HELENA You go so much backward when you fight.
>
> (I, i, 184–94)

I also refer the reader back to 'Melancholy Jaques' of *As You Like It*, who would withdraw 'under the shades of melancholy boughs'.

Renaissance astrologers describe planetary temperaments in a manner that is obviously not that of the modern psychological jargon dealing with personality. The evolution of language has also made their vocabulary semantically archaic, compared to character descriptions that can be found in the everyday speech of today.

However, it remains quite possible to test the validity of Renaissance planetary types by comparing them with the descriptions of the types that I have recently observed, using the rigorous methods of modern statistics (see Table 2, on p. 29).[7] In fact, the Renaissance astrologers and myself have adopted a parallel approach:

- we have used traits of character as the basic element for description;
- we have considered that each planetary type consists of clusters of traits;
- finally, we have maintained that a person possesses a given temperament when the planet which corresponds to this temperament is *dominant* in his or her horoscope.

Of course, our terminology differs when describing a *dominant* planet. In the Renaissance they speak of the 'Lord of the Geniture', whereas I talk of planets positioned in the rising and culminating Gauquelin 'plus zones' (see Figure 2, on p. 27). It is probable that there is not a perfect *astronomical* agreement between my definition of the dominant planet and that of the Renaissance, but this is only a secondary point. What is fundamental is that I have been able to show that the psychological attributes given to planets by Renaissance astrologers were — with a few exceptions — confirmed by my observations.

It is a surprising fact. Astrologers of that period were quite indifferent to objective verification: they repeated old recipes and more or less copied from each other, whereas empirical testing was my first concern. Nevertheless, the facts are here. I shall now demonstrate how I arrived at this conclusion.

The difficulties attached to seeing my project through were numerous. They especially concerned research and the choice of astrological *material*. Not all books written by Renaissance astrologers have survived to our day. Some have disappeared, others have been destroyed. The majority are still in Latin, and have not yet been translated into English. In any case, the originals are very difficult to get hold of, since they are rare and never leave the vaults of the large libraries. I must mention here that the numbers of works translated into English is increasing, thus making them more accessible to investigation. Nevertheless, the proportion that has not been translated, or simply not reprinted, still remains considerable. At

Children of the Planets

any rate, it was not my wish to spend too much of my time on studying these books; I was more anxious to preserve my objectivity as far as possible, and to do this, I preferred not to be the one extracting the traits of character from these often involved and verbose works. The ideal was to find a document in which some expert had published a synthesis of the question.

By chance, or, should I say, by searching in library files with an often physically unbearable sense of frustration, I discovered the work which suited my purpose: *Tamburlaine's Malady and Other Essays on Astrology in Elizabethan Drama*, by Johnstone Parr (1953). In this remarkable work of scholarship, Parr, professor of Renaissance history at the University of Alabama, brilliantly defends the thesis that Elizabethan drama – including the work of Shakespeare – is peppered with precise allusions to astrology. According to him the authors of this period show an astonishing knowledge of astral tradition, a tradition likewise known to the informed members of the audience, enabling them to appreciate the astrological allusions referring to characters in the play.

Almost all the chapters in Parr's book interested me, but I decided to concentrate on chapter 4, 'Astrology Motivates a Comedy', which deals solely with the question of the seven planetary types, presented in a schematic, but satisfactory way: 'The courtly circle of Elizabethan theatre-goers probably took exceptional notice when John Lyly personified the seven planets and employed them as the *modus operandi* of his comedy, *The Women in the Moone*,' writes Parr. He goes on to summarize the plot:

> In Lyly's play the shepherds of Utopia petition Nature to create for them a woman comrade, and Nature endows her creation, Pandora, with all the excellencies of the gods and goddesses in heaven. The seven planets, however, are envious because they have not been consulted in Pandora's creation, and accordingly determine to work her ruin. Each of the planets in turn attempts to bring about Pandora's undoing by subjecting her to its particular influence. Thereupon all of Pandora's actions and relations with the shepherds, caused by these planetary influences, form the simple plot of Lyly's play.[8]

This amusing plot became my passion because Parr had the idea of comparing the 'character' of each planet according to Lyly with the opinion of the most famous astrologers of the Elizabethan or preceding period. He concludes: 'The qualities which Lyly assigns rather carefully and painstakingly to each of the seven planets and the effects which they produce on Pandora, are in general those which have been admitted by competent astrologers.'[9] However, mention must be made of a bias that stressed the 'negative' rather than the 'positive' aspects of the planets. This is understandable, for in Lyly's play they are dissatisfied with Nature for creating Pandora and therefore try to upset her by forcing upon her their 'bad' sides. However, this does not change the *general tonality* of each planet, its deeper symbolism, which is what interests me most here. For example, when Saturn 'ascends' to 'signorize awhile' over Pandora, in Lyly's play, it is explained in this way:

> I shall instill such melancholy moode,
> As by corrupting of her purest blood,
> Shall first with sullen sorrowes clowde her braine
> And then surround her heart with forward care:
> She shall be sick with passion of the heart,
> Selfwild, and toungtide, but full fraught with teares.
>
> (I, i, 144–9)

Clearly, the melancholic Saturnine temperament that I have described at length is faithfully represented here. Parr is right in saying that Lyly had an excellent knowledge of what was to be found in the astrological textbooks of the period. Another witness, Jupiter, the next planet 'to ascend' cries out:

> Now Jupiter shall rule Pandora's thoughts,
> And fill her with Ambition and Disdaine;
> I will inforce my influence to the worst
> Lest other Planets blame my regiment.
>
> (II, i, 2–5)

And immediately, Pandora's mood changes:

> Though rancor now be rooted from my heart,
> I feel it burdened in an other sort:

Children of the Planets

> By day I think of nothing but of rule,
> By night my dreames are all of Empery.
> Mines eares delight to heare of Soveraigntie,
> My tongue desires to speak of princely sway,
> My eye would every object were a crowne.
>
> (II, i, 6–12)

As Parr remarks:

> Jupiter must indeed 'inforse' his influence 'to the worst', for all astrologers generally assign to Jupiter more benevolent influences than these ... But if unfortunately situated, Jupiter could be somewhat malicious. Thus Lyly is justified in maintaining that even the benefic Jupiter's influence could be detrimental, causing one to become haughty, overly ambitious, and commanding.[10]

And above all, Lyly draws very clearly the fundamental opposition between the temperaments of Saturn and Jupiter. It is not by chance that, in order to make his comedy racier, he brings Jupiter back on stage, just after Saturn has left. Albohazen Haly, for instance, notes: 'Jupiter abhors Saturn and his nature, prohibits and restrains him in all his works.'[11] The change of character here is most dramatic and must have greatly amused the audience, all 'knowledgeable' in the field of astrology and perfectly capable of understanding the finer points of the intrigue.

I refer the reader again to Parr who deals with the five other planets, or to one of my other works, *Cosmic Influences on Human Behavior*.[12] These two examples suffice to show that the text of *The Woman in the Moone*, accompanied by numerous quotations from astrologers provided by Parr, represent an excellent test to judge the 'scientific' value of Renaissance planetary signatures by. For each planet, I have not only short psychological descriptions taken from Lyly's comedy but, above all, interpretations – in terms of traits of character – taken from fourteen astrologers: Albumasar, Alchabitius, Augier Ferrier, Cornelius Agrippa, William Lilly, Albohazen Haly, Bartholomeus Anglicus, Guido Bonatti, the pseudo-Hermes Trismegistus, John Indagine, Claudius Dariot, Abraham Ibn Ezra, Jean-Baptiste Porta and Erra Pater.[13]

*

I noted all the traits of character relating to each planet and thus collected 1,500 cases of Renaissance traits. I then tested the validity of this material in the following manner.

The description of each planetary signature was compared to our catalogue of 50,000 traits.[14] For Jupiter, for example, Parr provides a list of traits: 'eloquence, magnanimitie, pryde, tyranny, wysedome, [etc.]', maybe 300 trait-units in all, and the majority of these traits were to be found in our catalogue. For each of the registered traits, we had the position of Jupiter at the birth of people to whom this trait was attributed in our biographical lists. All this work was objectively carried out several years before I had undertaken my present research. By now examining the traits described by Renaissance astrologers in this manner, I am able to establish the frequency of appearance of Jupiter in any position at the birth of all those who have 'astrological' Jupiterian traits. If it is found that Jupiter is frequently present in the Gauquelin 'plus zones', the regions of the sky where Jupiter is dominant (see Figure 2, p. 27), the astrologers will be proved to be correct in their views, and this will confirm our previous observations.

Naturally, I have applied the method described here for Jupiter to other planets. I was helped in the calculations by a programme which was especially designed by *Astro-Computing-Services*, from San Diego, California. The results of my work, published in 1982 in the journal *Correlation*,[15] seem to favour the theory of planetary signatures as seen by Renaissance man. In terms of traits of character, the celebrities in my professional groups were born more often than chance would permit with 'the right planet in the right place', that is to say in the Gauquelin 'plus zones', which probably correspond in part to the old-fashioned formulae: 'when a planet "Ascends", to "signorize awhile"', or 'The Lord of Geniture'. In short, my work demonstrates that the planetary temperaments, as conceived by Renaissance astrologers, have a scientific basis. Such an important conclusion deserves to be clarified, and also, slightly tempered.

Firstly, the results were positive for Mars, Jupiter, Saturn, Venus and the Moon. For the Sun and Mercury temperaments, they were negative. This was where Renaissance astrologers erred in attributing astral influences, like their colleagues in antiquity. Let me here remind the reader that in my work on the relation between occupations and traits of character, I have never been able to find evidence of the Sun or Mercury exerting any kind of astrological influence. There is a disturbing paradox here. How can we explain the 'absence' of these two planets in my work, when the temperaments attributed to them are historically as old and as specific as that of the others? It is a mystery.

Nevertheless, Renaissance astrologers, like others, are not always right. It should certainly not be overlooked that in this book I have separated the wheat from the chaff, and that I have shown an obvious bias in favour of astrological 'wheat'. This partiality is in my view entirely justified. It is the existence of the 'grain of gold' which is important. Without it, astrology can only be a long fairy tale. With it, it is a doctrine, albeit imperfect, which contains one of the secrets of the Universe that concerns us all. Without the 'grain of gold', no Copernican revolution can be possible for astrology. With it, this revolution is imminent, for, if astrologers have stumbled upon the truth, astronomers did so before them.

It is difficult to tear oneself away from the fascination exerted by the Renaissance period. It was an era of great changes and great discoveries. One would have liked it to succeed even further for example, by achieving a Copernican revolution in astrology. But the time had not yet come. Nevertheless, great minds tried to 'purify' the doctrine, like Kepler in rejecting the concept of 'houses'. The accent that was put on the angles of the sky, on planetary signatures, was already remarkable; even more remarkable is the notion of revaluation of an astrological type through an internal personal revolution. 'The planets are in us,' wrote Paracelsus. There were two main causes to the Renaissance failure. The first was the absence of a coherent theory to explain astral influences on man – a theory similar to the universal law of gravity but encompassing the planetary effect on man's behaviour. The second was

Neo-Astrology

the lack of rigorous empirical research in the modern sense; but birth data were rare and probability calculus non-existent.

For Arthur Koestler, the great astronomer-astrologers of the Renaissance were *sleepwalkers*, hence the title of his famous work. To my mind they were, above all, *tightrope walkers*. They walked the rope connecting antiquity and modern times without falling, sustained by the fragile balance of astrological tradition, but still listening to the 'music of the spheres'. Thus, while gazing at the sky and sitting next to Jessica, Shylock's daughter, Lorenzo explains to her what universal harmony is:

> Sit Jessica, – look how the floor of heaven
> Is thick inlaid with patens of bright gold,
> There's not the smallest orb which thou behol'st
> But in his motion like an angel sings,
> Still quiring to the young-eye'd cherubins:
> Such harmony is in immortal souls,
> But whilst this muddy vesture of decay
> Doth grossly close it in, we cannot hear it.
>
> (V, i, 58–65)

ACT FIVE

The Twentieth Century

I   Mars, the Bringer of War;
II   Venus, the Bringer of Peace;
III   Mercury, the Winged Messenger;
IV   Jupiter, the Bringer of Jollity;
V   Saturn, the Bringer of Old Age.

The Planets, op. 32,
Gustav Holst (1874–1934)

11

THE TROJAN HORSE

For its enemies, astrology is like the Hydra of Lerna, the monstrous octopus with numerous tentacles that Hercules had to face to accomplish one of his twelve labours. Each time Hercules managed to cut off one of the tentacles, another would grow, once more ready to strangle its adversary. The fight between the monster and the hero was long and dramatic. The hero, we know, managed to summon up enough strength to defeat and finally slay the beast. For its opponents, astrology is even more redoubtable than the Hydra of Lerna, because, in spite of the attacks that it has suffered for over two thousand years, it is still very much alive. Although it was thought dead in the nineteenth century, it has re-emerged here in the twentieth century more popular than ever. For its defenders, astrology is comparable to the Phoenix that rises again from its ashes, to shine once more like a fire-bird. But let us now leave these mythological comparisons.

At the end of his book, *Astrology and Alchemy: Two Fossil Sciences*, Mark Graubard includes a graph (reproduced here in Figure 10), accompanied by the following comment:

> The object of this graph is to summarize briefly the historical vicissitudes of . . . astrology. The description of the ordinate as 'Extent of Belief among the Learned' is approximate. It is measured by the number of treatises published on the subject and by its acceptance among diverse authors of the period. Note that astrology swept into Greece despite opposition, but did respond to Christian opposition and apathy, immediately following the teachings of the Bible. After the Revival of Learning in the tenth and eleventh centuries, Christian

Neo-Astrology

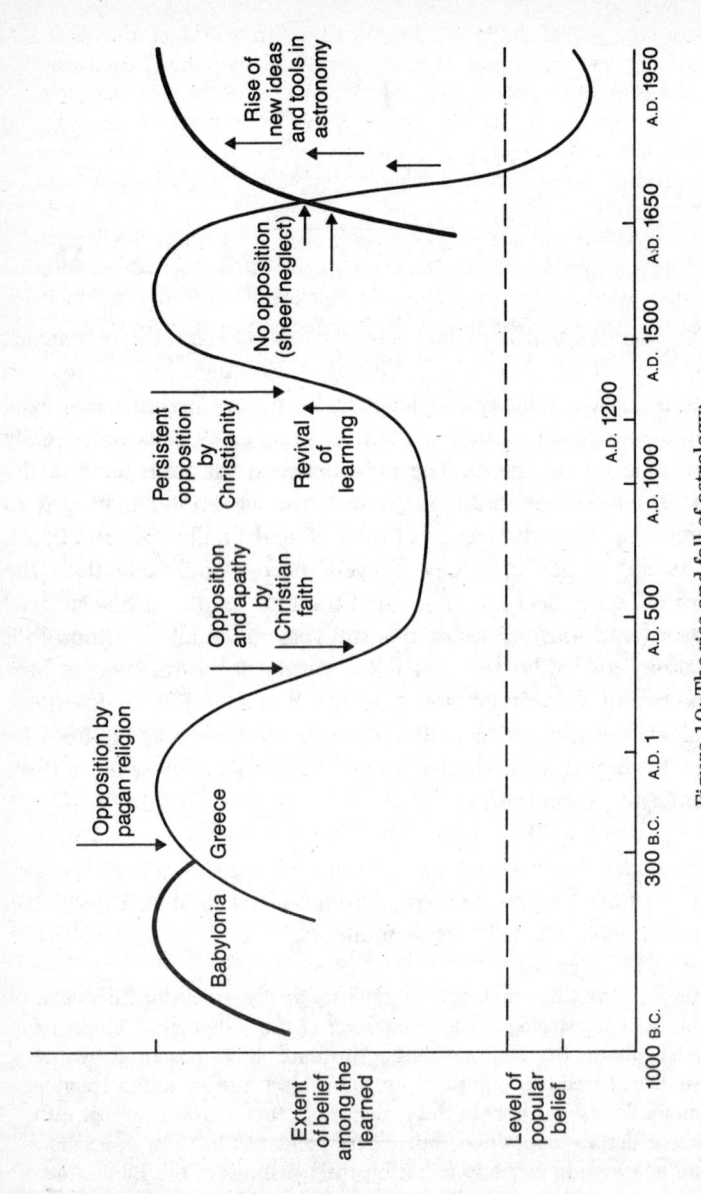

Figure 10: The rise and fall of astrology:
Modified (reduced) graph adapted from M. Graubard, *Astrology and Alchemy, Two Fossil Sciences* (1953).

The Trojan Horse

> opposition proved futile ... In the Christian world of the west, astrology reached its peak at the precise time when the Church was at the peak of its power. Yet, apparently, love of the new learning and the impact of fashion proved within the minds of the very supporters and rulers of the Church that the inherited prejudices against the materialistic and deterministic science come down from a pagan world.
>
> Note again that astrology's second decline, in the seventeenth century, occurs for entirely different reasons than its first fall into desuetude in the fourth century or thereabouts. The forces which obscured or repressed astrology earlier were absorption with religious values, while the forces which caused astrology's abandonment in the later period were equally enthusiastic absorption with the newly won scientific hypothesis, and the experimental zeal they generated.
>
> The level of popular belief was located on the graph in an arbitrary fashion merely to indicate that the astrological folklore is universal and deep-seated among people everywhere, regardless of its rise and fall among the learned. In the nineteenth century the popular level was significantly depressed but rose again in the turbulent and frustrating years of the mid-twentieth.[1]

The graph and analysis published by Graubard in 1953 are open to discussion, but I think they are pretty accurate. It may even be that the 'Extent of Belief among the Learned' has appreciably increased since Graubard's graph. Nevertheless, I feel that my comparison between astrology and the Hydra of Lerna is particularly appropriate in the light of this graph. Do we not see astrology growing, on several occasions, new tentacles to strangle Reason?

However, *belief* in astrology is one thing, and its scientific demonstration, the proof that it is *more* than just a belief but also a *reality* of Nature, is another.

At the turn of the century, in 1899 to be precise, the historian of astrology, Bouché-Leclercq, respected member of the Institut de France, formally rejected this possibility: 'Astrology is a faith which speaks the language of science, and a science which cannot find justification of its principles in faith.'[2] I will show that, on the contrary, even as Bouché-Leclercq was pronouncing these words, the material conditions were at last being gathered to give astrology a new chance: one century later, at the dawn of the year 2000, it is finally achieving its own 'Copernican revolution'.

No discovery can take place before its time, before a particular stage of social organization, technical progress and evolution of ideas has been reached. Discovering the 'grain of gold' in astrology requires that several material conditions exist concurrently, which has only recently been achieved: the creation of precise birth records; the publication of numerous biographical documents; the invention of probability calculus and its application in statistics; the advent of scientific psychology, and in particular the interest shown in the study of the personality.

The discovery of the 'grain of gold' also necessitates that there be sufficient motivation to seek it and, therefore, that astrology finds a large enough audience among the educated public. At the end of the twentieth century, the time is ripe for an *astrological* Renaissance – a situation comparable to that of *astronomy* in the sixteenth century.

The actual Copernican revolution was not accomplished solely as a result of the publication of Copernicus' work. In fact, as Thomas Kuhn has shown in his book on the subject, it was the scholars who succeeded Copernicus who completed the revolution he had started[3] and it is through their own discoveries, that they were able to impose his ideas. However, the Copernican revolution is only a scientific theory. A completely *different way of viewing the world* crumbled under the blows of Kepler and Galileo, although despite their genius, neither of them would have succeeded had technical progress not taken place in their time. Without the observations, of a precision unequalled at the time, of the Danish astronomer Tycho Brahe (1546–1601), Kepler would not have realized that the planets revolve around the Sun in ellipses, and not circles, as had been believed since Ptolemy's time; nor would he have set out the three laws of movement which carry his name. Without the invention of the telescope, Galileo would not have seen Jupiter's satellites, thereby facing the world with an inevitable conclusion: like the satellites revolving around Jupiter, the Earth *must* revolve around the Sun.

The Trojan Horse

In the sixteenth century, the idea of a Copernican revolution was 'in the air'. In the twentieth century, it is the notion of 'scientific' astrology that is 'in the air'. A number of factors favour its acceptance.

In 1793, a decree of the Public Welfare Committee (Comité de Salut Public), issued in Year I of the French Republic, made compulsory for all citizens to declare the birth of a child within three days to the civil authorities, and to specify not only the day but also the *time* of birth.

This was a landmark for astrology. Thanks to the French Revolution, we now have in France birth registers specifying the time and date that go back almost two centuries. Although a large part of my life as been spent in the dusty archives of numerous cities, searching through these documents has always filled me with delight. Even today, I am amazed to discover in these old registers, written in old-fashioned handwriting faded by time, the date of birth of a person I am searching for. Indeed, these birth registers have been my 'Galileo's telescope'.

Of course, the French Revolution also produced Napoleon I, who conquered a large part of Europe and forced upon it – when he had the time – the civil code which bears his name. Consequently, Belgium, Holland, Germany on the west bank of the Rhine, and what used to be the Kingdom of Naples in Italy, have all been including the time of birth in their registers since 1810! The fact that Napoleon I never conquered England (and was finally defeated by it) might, in this respect, be considered a setback for astrology. Even today, English astrologers despair of ever seeing the day when Her Majesty's government will pass a bill requiring the time of birth to be added in birth records (only independent-minded Scotland has been including it since 1850).

Even after his death, the good seed sown by Napoleon gradually bore fruit elsewhere in Europe: all of Italy in 1866, and all of Germany – Greater Germany – in 1876, began to include the time in birth registers. The United States followed, but later, at the beginning of the twentieth century.

Neo-Astrology

These millions of recorded times constitute an indispensable treasure trove for the researcher. The position of planets in relation to the horizon and meridian cannot be calculated, and it is therefore impossible to know if they are in the Gauquelin 'plus zones' or not, without knowing the time of birth.

I have never taken the time to go into the minutes of the Public Welfare Committee's deliberations of 1793. I would, however, very much like to know the name of the Revolutionary who had the idea of enforcing the inclusion of the time of birth on birth certificates. He was one of astrology's benefactors.

It is also necessary to decide on the persons whose time of birth we would like to find out. For this, it is indispensable to know certain facts: their profession and family situation, to begin with, as well as the time and place of their birth.

Formerly, the only well-documented births were those of the children of persons in high places. For others, one had to resort to guesswork. Fortunately, in the nineteenth century – thanks to social progress – biographical documentation, previously very scanty, became more extensive. Works on famous people in different occupations were published, providing indispensable reference material regarding the place and date of birth and death of the great painters, scientists, generals, etc., of each country, with details of events in their lives and of traits of character. In France, one of the first complete books of biographies of French notables was published in 1890 by Virolleaud: it listed thousands of names. Since then, this type of publication has multiplied, and there is a *Who's Who* for almost every country in the world and every category of people.

All this enables us to set up extensive investigations based on reliable material. Let us recall Vettius Valens, and his collection of 139 horoscopes with which to prove astrology, or even Guido Bonatti who, in the seventeenth century, succeeded in collecting 329 and imagine for a moment that they lived in the twentieth century: might they not have been capable of collecting several thousand cases and of defending the cause of astrology much better than they did? After all, they knew intuitively that only the study of

The Trojan Horse

a great number of horoscopes could provide proof of the truth of their convictions.

However, their convictions in themselves wouldn't have sufficed. They would still have needed to know exactly what is meant by 'a great number'. Probability calculus did not really develop until the nineteenth century, especially with the work of Carl Gauss (1777–1855). Statistics applied to natural phenomena are even more recent. The first rumblings of demography, for example, started in mid-nineteenth century. Adolphe Quételet, a Belgian doctor, was the first to study the distribution of the numbers of births according to the hours of a day. His material was the 2,680 births which occurred in the Saint-Pierre Hospital in Brussels, between 1811 and 1822.[4] He showed, *inter alia*, that children are more often born in the morning than the afternoon, a discovery which was very useful in my research.

Even if they had been in possession of such a large number of correctly registered birth data, Vettius Valens and Guido Bonatti would still have lacked knowledge of the meaning of words such as: *average, variance, threshold of significance, control group* – to mention only a few fundamental statistical notions. (I will later demonstrate that even in the twentieth century, for that matter, it is not enough to have scientific instruments at one's disposal, one must put them to good use.)

In order to make their astronomical calculations, these authors also lacked tables of planetary positions as perfected and precise as the ones we have today. Moreover, until Placidus and even after him, many authors – starting with Vettius Valens himself – got slightly muddled when calculating the limits of astrological houses.

It is only since the turn of the twentieth century that astronomical ephemerides – especially designed for astrological use – have been published, such as Raphaël's in England and Paul Choisnard's in France. They have proved, however, somewhat insufficient for research purposes. For my part I have had to do by hand astronomical calculations for births earlier than 1850, using Choisnard's tables which gave the planetary positions only every ten days! In the 1990s, the lucky owner of a personal computer, who needs

147

simply to press a key to know the planetary positions from 2000 B.C. to A.D. 2000 and beyond, can appreciate the difference.

The advent of modern psychology was also among the conditions which allowed a better approach to astrological phenomenon. Especially significant was the progress made in the domain of the psychology of personality. It was not so long ago that psychology was confused with philosophy and that its study relied on words, not facts. Until quite recently whatever talk there was of memory, attention to ideas, sensation, was without an empirical basis. In order to pass my *baccalauréat* in 1948, I had to grasp Bergson's subtle conception of memory. This is not to say that Bergson is without interest, but his is a philosophy in the guise of psychology, with no practical application.

Fortunately, in the 1930s, Anglo-Saxon researchers rediscovered the notion of traits of character and of the structure of personality, which is a good foundation for an empirical approach to human behaviour. In 1936, the American psychologists, G. Allport and H. Odbert, published a monograph which remains a classic, in which they list 17,953 words in the English language that describe traits of character. In their preface, the authors explained the relevance of their work, which subsequently was, in fact, the departure point for several important studies:

> Sooner or later, every psychologist working in the field of personality collides with the problem of traits-names. Whatever method he employs, he is forced to ask himself if the terms he is using in describing qualities and attributes of personality do actually denote psychic dispositions or traits, or whether these terms are mischievious verbal snares tempting him into the pitfalls or peril of 'verbal magic'.[5]

I have said above that contemporary psychologists had 'rediscovered' this because it was Greek astrologers who actually invented astral psychology, and Renaissance astrologers who developed it. The contemporary psychologist has only taken the torch from the astrologer's hand. For example, in 1940, an American psychologist, W. Sheldon, worked on the correlation between physical constitution and psychological type, something which resembles the astro-

The Trojan Horse

logical theory of Hippocrates' and Galen's 'humours'.[6] In the same way, Hans Eysenck's research on the dimensions of the personality is not without similarity to some of the notions current during antiquity.[7] In astrology, the notion of traits of character allows the stress in a horoscope to be put on psychology, rather than luck or than a misfortune caused by a fatal destiny. Every serious astrologer today knows this.

Nevertheless, all these recent contributions would have come to nothing had there not been an astonishing renewal of interest in astrology at the dawn of the twentieth century. This renewal was part of a broader movement towards the study of 'occult sciences', and especially of theosophy. From the turn of the century, astrological publications began multiplying. In England, Alan Leo created a society and started a magazine which gained many followers; in France, in 1897, Fomalhaut (the pseudonym of Abbé Nicolaud), wrote the *Traité d'astrologie sphérique et judiciaire* (Treaty of Spherical and Judiciary Astrology). In this work, Fomalhaut repeated, almost point by point, Ptolemy's *Tetrabiblos*, but he deserves credit for having rediscovered it. He also published detailed instructions on how to calculate the tables of houses according to Placidus.

The facts are here: at the beginning of the twentieth century, educated minds – and, it goes without saying, others who were less so – once again turned their attention to astrology, and prepared, with the zeal of novices, to inject it with fresh blood. The discovery of three new planets – Uranus, Neptune and, later, Pluto – that had been unknown to the ancients, excited the imagination.

Everything, then, was in place for the curtain to rise and reveal a new character: 'scientific' astrology, anxious to return with honours to the bosom of Science which had banished it three centuries earlier. But who would give the signal for the curtain to rise? Without being chauvinistic, I believe the Frenchman Paul Choisnard did so.

To demonstrate that a doctrine is well-founded when it cannot be justified through an acceptable physical mechanism, it is necessary to address the problem indirectly, in a roundabout way, since it cannot be resolved in a direct fashion. I was going to say: 'by a ruse', Statistics are the 'Trojan Horse' which will make it possible to penetrate the astrological citadel, until then unassailable.

This, for instance, was the approach taken by Paul Broca – the famous physician who discovered the motor speech centre in the brain.[8]

Broca tried to provide a statistical basis for the theory that the most intelligent people have the largest brain. He measured hundreds of skulls, but consequently admitted with admirable honesty that his measurements had been biased by his unconscious desire to obtain results to justify his theory.[9] Because it is not, of course, enough simply to apply statistics; it needs to be done correctly.

At the end of the last century, when parapsychology – then called 'metaphysics' – aroused great enthusiasm, Charles Richet suggested applying probability calculus to paranormal phenomena. Richet was a very respected figure, a Nobel Prize winner in medicine, and his suggestion was followed up. In the United States, J. B. Rhine later applied it on a large scale.

As for Choisnard, he did take up the idea of using probability calculus, but this time it was for the benefit of astrology.[10]

12

UNFORTUNATE FORERUNNERS

It has rightly been stated that science's principal aim should be to establish categories of natural phenomena. The categories of astrology are the numerous elements of the horoscope: the signs of the zodiac, planets, aspects, houses, etc. Instead of judging the value of a horoscope globally, we can try to take apart the mechanism, to verify one by one, the laws on which it rests. In this way, we shall be applying a method of analysis whose success had been proved in all the natural sciences.

Probability calculus is relatively recent, although authors in earlier times did not lack statistical intuition. A layman in this field, even a king, may also be gifted with this type of intuition, as the following anecdote shows.

Madame du Hausset, chambermaid to Madame de Pompadour, favourite of Louis XV, reports on the king's attitude to astrology. She recounts that Madame de Pompadour once went to see 'a sorceress', who charted her horoscope:

> Madame told the king about the curiosity she had had, and he laughed about it saying that he would have liked the police to have arrested her; but he also added a very sensible thing: 'To be able to judge the truth or falsity of such predictions, it is necessary to assemble about fifty; it would be seen that similar sentences are almost always used and that they sometimes lack any relevance, sometimes apply to the subject; but people do not talk about the former, only the latter.'[1]

It is not the king's scepticism which I shall dwell on here, but his idea that 'to judge the truth or falsity of such predictions it is necessary to assemble about fifty'.

Neo-Astrology

Paul Choisnard (1867–1930), a graduate of the prestigious École Polytechnique Française, spent most of his life trying to prove the scientific reality of astrology. He set out his principles in his work *Langage Astral*, where he considered, first of all, what he called 'the false treatises':

> I call 'false treatises' the 'manuals of divination' that lack critical, logical and methodical sense, and evidence; their authors, who teach a 'doctrine', imagining that they have proved a rule as soon as they pronounce it, and have a few examples to support it (always easy to find), believe they are exempt from distinguishing between *coincidence* and the application of a *law*. This is how we have accumulated, since antiquity, the most arbitrary rules. These remarks justify provisionally *limiting* to *essential notions* the study which is here presented. But should one proceed by trial and error in order to bring out the 'essential' in these notions, as I have done for quite a long time and in an epoch (end of nineteenth century) when the only things to enlighten us were the writings of the Middle Ages or the divinatory manuals simply copied from them, with a surcharge of almost useless calculations? At the beginning of this century, scientific astrology *had not yet been born.*[2]

For Choisnard it is only the establishment of several precise laws that matters. He is against 'collectors of rules',[3] adding: 'astrologers always speak in the name of "experiment", but never define it.'[4] He opposes any occult aspect of astrology: 'as for a *symbology* that is created from illusory and unverifiable correspondences – it is not necessary to discuss it here – those who support it shy away from all logic and even any definition . . . Occultism has no more reason to claim astrology than chemistry, radio or electricity.'[5]

And he concludes his Introduction with these words: 'If the study of *ancient astrology* reveals that basically there is very little in it that is true, it is at least necessary to be able to prove this fact. In any case, it will always remain useful to calm the untimely ardour of neologists and deniers.'[6] In other words, astrology must contain a 'grain of gold'; it is up to me, Choisnard, to find and prove its existence with the aid of statistics. There is not much to add to these principles of strict obedience to science. In his many works, Choisnard states various statistical laws, thus establishing, in his opinion, the reality of the astrological fact, summarized in particular in *Preuves et bases de l'astrologie scientifique* (The Proof and Basis of Scientific Astrology), published in 1921.[7]

When my friend, Aimé Durand, and I played truant at the Lycée Charlemagne so that we could go to old Monsieur Chacornac's astrological store on the Seine embankment, just opposite the cathedral of Notre-Dame, it was definitely not Choisnard's work which interested us the most. At the back of his cramped and dark headquarters, his head covered with a fur cap, his bloated red face buried in the old papers which covered his table, Chacornac appeared to be asleep. At the time, Aimé and I were more fascinated by the works of those 'collectors of rules' that Choisnard rightly denounced. True, we were only sixteen years old. My 'Astrological Treatise', written on school paper during the never-ending hours of maths or Latin, while sitting hidden at the back of the class under Aimé's protection, does not mention Choisnard – for the simple reason that I had not yet read his work, put off by the difficulty of the abstract principles he proposed.

Some time later, I decided to make the necessary effort, and was very *impressed* as soon as I properly understood what I was reading. All of a sudden, Aimé and I became Choisnard enthusiasts, set on succeeding him. It was about the same time that Aimé, very excited, arrived at my place one day, carrying a copy of the enormous *Traité d'astrobiologie* (Astrobiological Treatise) by Karl Ernst Krafft, as thick and heavy as a brick. Published in 1939, but out of print and impossible to find in the shops since the end of the war, it was a book shrouded in mystery and legend. Aimé had unearthed it at one of the bookstalls along the Seine embankment, so well known to the tourists.

Krafft's book, in its dull, unattractive brown cover, was much more involved and complex than Choisnard's works, but with its figures and graphs, closely printed in small type, it impressed us even more. It was as a result of this that Aimé and I, in the years of 1949 and 1950, began writing to registrars and archives in the main cities of France to obtain the times of birth of famous people and so draw up their horoscopes. Our requests had increased at such an alarming rate, that we were immediately asked by the guardians of these precious documents to slow down the pace of our demands. Engrossed in his studies, Aimé subsequently abandoned the research and I continued alone. Nevertheless, he never lost his interest in it. Twenty years later, it was entirely due to his material assistance that we were able to publish the series of large volumes of birth data in my laboratory.

One of my priorities was to repeat Choisnard's experiments. The unfortunate man seemed to have preached in the wilderness all his life in the hope of gaining recognition for his 'laws' in the scientific world. Was Choisnard, twenty years after his death, about to receive his consecration thanks to me? I sincerely hoped so.

In *L'influence des astres* (The Influence of the Stars), I presented the detailed results of my efforts to try to confirm Choisnard's rules, alas, without ever succeeding to do so.[8] (I will not go into them here as they are rather technical and have already been published.[9]) On the other hand, Choisnard's work deserves more than a passing comment if I am to apply to it the same criteria which I have used in this book and have applied to his predecessors.

First of all, Choisnard's failure is rather puzzling. How could he fail with such good principles? I think he could not have known how to apply them to his own research. Curiously, he was, in fact, unaware of the statistical law of deviation from the norm. Working only with the aid of the primitive method of percentages and on small groups of two to three hundred cases at the most, he soon lost his way. Above all, a psychological block prevented him from truly wiping the slate clean of Ptolemy's tradition, which he often accepted *de facto*, and from starting from scratch, as was his intention. In his basic work *Langage astral* he gives a 'recapitulatory table of the elements for interpretation of the sky at birth'.[10] In his table, he then lists a whole series of 'general laws of influences', which are, all in all, very classical. One only needs to refer to an astrological manual to realize this. None of these 'laws', though, have been

Unfortunate Forerunners

empirically proved by him, which is an inconsistency on the part of someone who claimed to keep strictly to 'a small number of well-proven facts'. The weight of 'astral' belief brought down the barrier of Choisnard's scientific principles. This is a pity, for his work was praiseworthy.

Forty years ago, when I saw Choisnard's claims disappear one after another under the weight of my painstaking calculations, I resented him for being the cause of my fruitless efforts and of the hopes I had entertained. This explains why I was unfair to him in my first book. Why unfair? Because Choisnard also carried the 'grain of gold' of astrology in his stock *without having proved it*. As he drew his inspiration from Ptolemy and Renaissance authors, like them he stressed three factors we have already encountered: the importance of the angles, astral psychology, and heredity.

In *Langage astral*, Choisnard writes:

> The *intensity* of the planet's rays obviously depends on its position in the astrological houses: *maximum intensity* corresponds to an area around the *meridian* and the *horizon* of around 10 degrees (in the cardinal or even cadent houses). The Midheaven and the Ascendant present the most important places in this respect. [Ptolemy asserts this in his *Tetrabiblos* – Book III, Chapter 3] and experience clearly confirms it ... Mars and Saturn in any of the four *angular* positions are bad. Jupiter and Venus are good ... The figure below represents the disposition of the houses in any chart; it accounts for relative intensity due to the houses. The density of the shading is proportional to this intensity (this law of intensity in astrological houses is verified through experiments).[11] [See Figure 11.]

What does Choisnard contribute that his predecessors have not already stated? Nothing, and in fact he does not claim otherwise. But he clearly stresses the 'angularities', which he calls 'maximum intensity' and positions very close to the Gauquelin 'plus zones'. This is a positive point. He is wrong, however, in his assertion that 'experiments clearly show' the fact that Mars and Saturn in angular positions are 'bad', and Jupiter and Venus, 'good'. This demonstrates that he has not set up a proper statistical inquiry into the houses. I

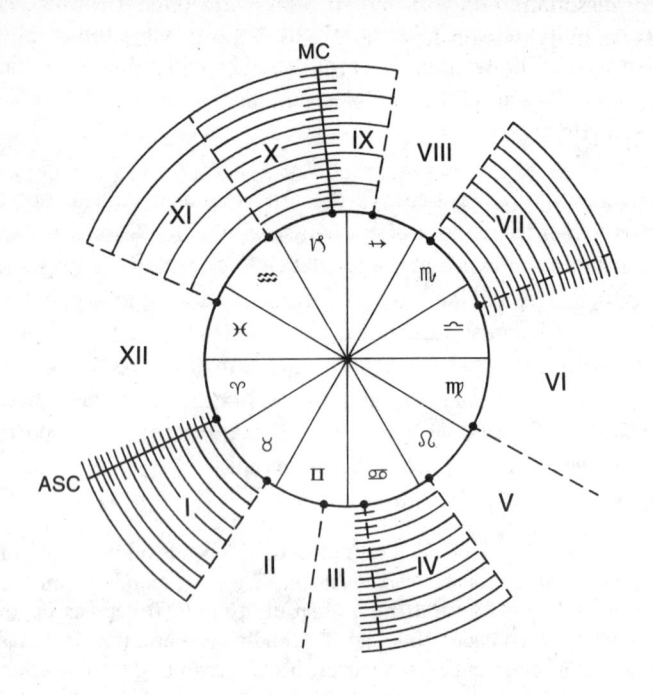

Figure 11: Planetary intensity in the houses according to Choisnard.

---

have observed that there are no 'good' or 'bad' *angular* planets: planets simply correspond to different tendencies. Choisnard was right in insisting on the importance of angular planets, but did not rectify the errors of the past.

In one of his other books, Choisnard includes a 'Dictionary of astral psychology for the interpretation of the sky at birth'.[12] In this dictionary, psychological correspondences are listed for each trait. Curiously, it begins with an element of destiny, 'accidents', linked

Unfortunate Forerunners

to the 'dissonant notes of Saturn, Mars and often Uranus'. Then comes 'activity', associated with 'a dominant Mars, especially in aspects with Mercury, the Moon and Uranus'. 'Self-esteem' is linked to 'exalted Jupiter in aspect with Saturn'. Kindness is associated with 'Jupiter and Venus forming a good aspect with the Moon'; etc.

We can also find, among other things, the Renaissance planetary temperaments. Here too, there are remarkable points of convergence with my observations (activity linked to Mars; self-esteem linked to Jupiter). The only novelty is the introduction of the planet Uranus, discovered by Herschel in 1781 and therefore not found in the psychological palette of ancient astrologers. To Uranus, Choisnard attributes accidents, independence, originality, eccentricity and a psychological judgement. But where is the proof?

Choisnard provides more interest when – in rendering homage to Kepler – he emphasizes planetary heredity. He did in fact, publish a book on this subject, *La Loi d'hérédité astrale* (The Law of Planetary Heredity), in which he makes the following summary: 'When comparing birthcharts two by two, many astrological factors show more frequent similarity between close relatives (father, mother, brothers and sisters), than between individuals with no kinship.'[13] And he adds a comment with which Kepler would have agreed:

> We must never forget that we are born under a particular sky, but at the same time, we are born under this sky because we have such predispositions, already sketched out by heredity and during gestation ... If, in fact, the planets at birth did not exert any influence and orientation on the newborn, the tendency on the part of nature to make a man be born under astral aspects analogous to those of his parents would not make any sense.[14]

In theory, this rather resembles some of my ideas on the question (which were in fact inspired by the reading of Choisnard). Unfortunately, *La Loi d'hérédité astrale* does not fulfil the hopes it arouses. The experimental proof comes to little. None of the work deals with *angularity* and the only striking statistic relates the heredity of certain positions in the signs of the zodiac. I have shown, though, that such zodiacal heredity does not exist.[15]

Neo-Astrology

There is, moreover, a lot of confusion in the ideas of Choisnard (and of Kepler) on the subject of planetary heredity. For them, to this planetary heredity is added an *external predestination*, which *also* comes from planets. According to Choisnard, we are born under a particular sky because it is in harmony with our tendencies, but, a strange turnabout, the sky itself, following a mysterious celestial sequence, in its turn causes good and bad periods in life. I am not far from believing that Choisnard's failure is due to this confusion, this mixture of two things so entirely opposed in their essence as heredity and predestination, which is external to heredity. How else can one reconcile the coherent hypothesis of planetary heredity with this astro-deterministic explanation of the fate of Robespierre (1758–94), a redoubtable figure of the French Revolution who ended on the guillotine: 'At the age of thirty-six, Robespierre was under the influence of an exceptional convergence of planetary discords, capable of causing the most violent storm possible in his chart. The play of bad rays between the significators of vitality and the malefic planets was exerting the maximum influence.'[16]

Choisnard stated that before him, 'scientific astrology *had not yet been born*'. The question is: What is left of it after him? In truth, the answer hardly matters. For me, Choisnard – whose work deserves the attention I have given it – was a source of disappointment, but also of inspiration, and I would like to preserve the inspiration. First of all, there is his application of statistics to astrology, and also his tables of planetary positions which are easy to use and were for a long time indispensable to my work. But perhaps more important than this, at the end of *Langage astral*, Choisnard includes a list of birth dates – not a very long one, it includes 200 dates at most – of famous people in different occupations, the time of birth having been taken from the registry office. Choisnard was, without doubt, the *first* to have had the idea of using this valuable source of information bequeathed to us by the Committee of Public Welfare. It was when using this list of dates and times of birth, followed by the magic sign 'e.c.' (a French abbreviation for *état-civil*, or registry office), that I got the idea of writing to those official sources myself and of modestly beginning my research. Thus, Choisnard was a courageous pioneer misled by Nature; but in his way – and more than any other – he handed down the 'grain of gold' to me.

Whereas Choisnard kept the word 'astrology', another researcher who, after him, made the most systematic attempt to 'reconstruct' the planetary influences, the Swiss, Karl Ernst Krafft, rejected the name and talked of *astrobiology*. Born in Basle, Switzerland, in 1900, Krafft could have been Choisnard's son. He explains his rejection of the word 'astrology', in *Traité d'astrobiologie* (Astrobiological Treatise):

> The very word *astrology* creates an attitude of mistrust that prevents any impartial examination of the facts, particularly since the authors in question did not sufficiently eliminate from their inquiries, traditional, unproven data, such as the notion of 'houses', 'aspects', etc. This is why we have adopted, without bias, methods of investigation that are perfectly objective ... Inspired by the desire to be impartial, the research and results set forth in this volume have become a challenge to those who persistently deny the astrobiological connections: for the credulous, who cling to current astrological traditions – it is a real disaster. All this, while proving the reality of cosmo- and astrobiological relations, as well as the fragility of so many premises and rules on which astrophiles of all continents and of all degrees of vulgarization thought they could rely![17]

These peremptory statements, these revolutionary and excellent principles, provide a confident introduction to the author's work, most of which is contained in the famous *Traité*, an enormous work that offers in statistical form a considerable amount of material proving the influence of planets. An impressive result in favour of astrology – *on the face of it.*

When my friend Aimé Durand showed me this book for the first time, leafing through it I experienced a feeling of admiration and developed a sort of inferiority complex. Aimé shared this view completely. Here, at last, was a man who spoke another language, rejected the word astrology, and filled the pages of his book with the most varied and unexpected results, in order to prove, at last, that astrology – in becoming *astrobiology* – had found its Copernicus. I confess to having once – it was a long time ago though! – promised myself to dedicate my first essays to the memory of the great Karl Ernst Krafft: today, I shudder at the thought!

It was indeed fierce determination that enabled me to penetrate this dense jungle of a book. However, armed with an immense desire to understand and some statistical knowledge just acquired at the university, to my great disappointment, I found myself compelled to topple my idol from his pedestal. His evidence, as it became clear, was based on erroneous reasoning from the statistical point of view. When tested – which I did on numerous occasions – it could not be confirmed by the new results. (I have since published a very detailed – almost page for page – criticism of Krafft's work in *L'Influence des astres*.[18] However, it is not my intention to deal with the issue again here.)

To my mind, this new setback was due less to technical errors, flagrant as these were, as to Krafft's personality. In his book *Le Monde étrange des astrologues* (The Strange World of Astrologers),[19] Ellic Howe has given a good description of the researcher, and of his blind confidence in himself and his work. Being pro-Nazi, during the second world war Krafft accepted a post in Berlin as translator of the prophecies of Nostradamus, for the benefit of Hitler's propaganda. But he did not prove amenable enough for his fearsome employers, who imprisoned and then deported him. He died of typhoid on his way to Buchenwald concentration camp in the winter of 1945. Krafft was a 'believer', who lost his way in the world of 'rationalist' researchers. This error is scarcely more forgivable in science, than his misguided decision to work for the Nazis.

This is all the sadder for his memory. In removing all tradition from his research in order to create a new, revolutionary concept, he did not even succeed – unlike Choisnard – in passing on to us the 'grain of gold' of astrology. Nothing remains of his work, because he willingly cut off the roots of a tradition several thousand years old. Nevertheless, some respects are due to the memory of this great but irrational worker.

*

Unfortunate Forerunners

Another not very rational author needs to be mentioned here. Léon Lasson, born in 1901 and, to my knowledge, still of this world in 1990. Marc Ruchet, a young astrologer friend, confided to me that Lasson claims that he will live to be one hundred and twenty! Lasson is an eccentric, to say the least, and does not shy from addressing the media and political leaders directly when he has urgent revelations on the future of our planet. For example, in 1969, he thought he saw sombre auguries in the close passage of Kohoutec's comet to the Earth and put together an 'open letter' to Mr Chaban-Delmas, at the time France's Prime Minister, and then bombarded the papers and people in high places with it. Having had the privilege of being on his mailing list, I too received this letter. It advised the French government to take immediately draconian measures: the third world war was imminent and millions of people would be mourned as a result of the passage of the Kohoutec comet. Cassandra herself could not have been more pessimistic. Lasson amassed the most dire apocalyptic predictions, followed by numerous exclamation marks! Fortunately, none of it occurred and Kohoutec's comet departed, not having harmed a fly.

Thirty years earlier, however, Lasson was much more optimistic. His first book, which appeared in 1938, was called *Astrologie mondiale: la loi des grands événements historiques: quinze ans de paix sur l'Europe* (World Astrology, the Law of Great Historical Events: Fifteen Years of Peace for Europe).[20] To have published a book in 1938 which announced fifteen years of peace in Europe was unfortunate, to say the least, since the second world war, that caused the deaths of millions of people, was to erupt the year after!

Later, Lasson was to surprise us again when he published, in 1954, *A la recherche des planètes transplutoniennes* (In Search of Transplutonian Planets).[21] He had discovered 'through intuition' several planets gravitating beyond the orbit of Pluto – the furthest away from the Sun and planets. He gave them names and endowed them with precise influences. For example, he mentioned a planet called Prosperpine, which was said to be the planet of homosexuality. He went even further and published the tables of positions for these hypothetical planets, adding a few statistics to boot to prove their influence. Needless to say, even with the help of space probes, astronomers have not observed any planets beyond Pluto.

The claims of this author should therefore be approached with great caution. The astrological community itself – usually quite open to the most audacious novelties – proved reluctant to follow Lasson. Disappointed, he announced in 1954 that he would henceforth remain silent. Like Achilles, he retired to his tent and, in fact, has not published anything since.

Why then mention here this eccentric character? Because of one of his other books, *Ceux qui nous guident* (Those Who Guide Us),[22] that appeared in 1946. The author defends within its pages yet another of his audacious theories: the way of numbering houses used by astrologers since the Greeks is incorrect! The number of each house should, according to him, be moved one space on in the direction of the diurnal movement. In this way, house XI becomes house XII, house X becomes XI, house IX becomes X, and so on.

This moves the angular houses, where the planets are traditionally strong, into the place previously occupied by the cadent houses, previously considered weak, following the direction of the diurnal movement. More specifically, Lasson states, the astrological house XII – positioned above the Ascendant and not below it – is in fact, the 'true' angular house I; in the same way, astrological house IX – positioned after the Midheaven and not before – is in fact the 'true' angular house number X. He makes the angular houses coincide, so to speak, with the regions in the sky where the Gauquelin 'plus zones' are situated. Now *this* is interesting. Even more so because, in defence of his theory, Lasson collected the birth data of several hundred people, divided up according to occupation, with which he claimed to obtain results. These groups are too small to have a statistical significance – some are made up of less than a hundred cases – but the graphs Lasson includes are suggestive. We frequently notice Mercury rising at the birth of writers, Venus for artists, Mars for military men, Uranus for politicians, Neptune for mystics.

I must say that when I discovered Lasson's work – a short time after having read and understood Choisnard – I was struck by the error of his method, above all in the statistical field. Shortly after

Unfortunate Forerunners

the book appeared, he was attacked on this point in *Les Cahiers Astrologiques* by Jean Hiéroz, one of the rare astrologers at the time capable of understanding probability calculus. Hiéroz demonstrated that Lasson's statistics 'were completely wrong and therefore without significance'.[23]

Lasson's neglect, or ignorance, of the roles of astronomical and demographic factors is even more serious. This error clearly explains some of the results that he published, and especially the fact that writers are born more often when Mercury is rising than chance would allow. He neglects here two phenomena I described in 1955, to wit the proximity of Mercury to the Sun, seen from Earth, and the fact that the majority of births occur in the morning. These two phenomena in combination *naturally* result in the above average occurrence of Mercury rising in *all* births, and not only those of writers. Lasson's mistake is all the more natural since writers have traditionally always been considered as 'the children of Mercury' (see Chapter 10). If we take into account the necessary adjustments of frequency, nothing is left of the Mercury effect on writers.

This error – among others – prompted my severe criticism of Lasson in *L'influence des astres*.[24] A short debate between Lasson and myself subsequently appeared in *Les Cahiers Astrologiques* of 1956, to which I refer the interested reader.[25]

Despite all this, and even because of my criticism, some astrologers became the champions of Lasson, in whom they saw the precursor of my work. To all those who claimed that I had confirmed Lasson's results, Geoffrey Dean replied:

> In fact, this is incorrect. A study[26] has compared the results of Lasson (based on 807 cases) and Gauquelin (based on 13,293 cases). For Lasson's six professional groups a total of eighteen planets are claimed to be significant by one or other author. But only four are in agreement, and of these three exhibit no significant correlation between their distributions; the fourth (Mars for military men) showed an individually significant correlation which, among eighteen distributions, is not significant. In other words, Gauquelin was not able to confirm Lasson's thesis.[27]

What is more, Lasson and myself do not speak the same language

Neo-Astrology

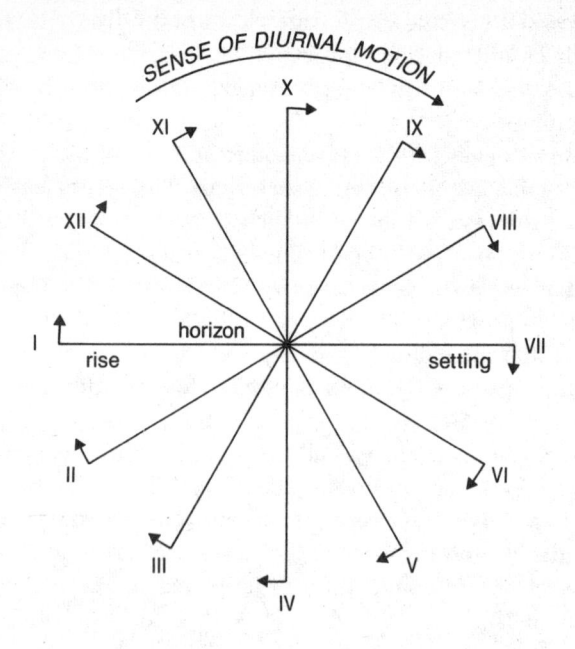

Figure 12: The twelve houses according to Lasson.

at all. In this connection, I refer the readers to Figure 12 (see above). The graph reproduced illustrates Lasson's lack of logic:

- He states that the boundary to each house marks the beginning of its zone of influence in the daily movement, clockwise – herein lies his originality.
- However, like all astrologers, he keeps the numbering of the twelve houses in the opposite direction to that of the daily movement, anticlockwise.
- He then proposes an absurd diagram of the order of houses, contrary to both astrological and astronomical logic.

Unfortunate Forerunners

The diagram would have been logical if, starting from the Ascendant, he had numbered the houses following the direction of the daily movement. This idea did not cross his mind: he firmly believed in the sequence of the twelve houses being in the opposite direction of the movement. Thus, a planet in house I, starting from the Ascendant, when rising towards its culmination, will remain in this house until it reaches the boundary of the following house, which happens to be ... house XII! The planet is in this way rising 'against the current', through houses XI, X, etc. Just as it does in classical astrology. Literally, Lasson only brought the houses forward by one slot. He keeps their numbers, the anticlockwise distribution, and their astrological influences.

I recently wrote:

> In fact, there is no meaningful resemblance between Lasson's 'shifted' houses and the Gauquelin 'plus zones'. The best proof was provided by Lasson himself in a work he published in 1954, i.e. eight years after the work I am speaking of, his *Traité d'astrologie moderne* [Treatise of Modern Astrology].[28] On page 52, he gives in the form of keywords, pompously labelled 'basic key ideas', his meaning of the twelve houses. For the edification of the reader, I reproduce below the twelve keywords *à la* Lasson. The roman numerals indicate the number of each house according to traditional astrology; the arabic numerals, those according to Lasson (who is a champion of the Regiomontanus system of house division, and not of the more astronomically accurate Placidus system):

I	2 possessions	VII	8 reflexes
II	3 thoughts	VIII	9 expansion
III	4 instincts	IX	10 accomplishments
IV	5 influence	X	11 images
V	6 exchanges	XI	12 emotions
VI	7 sensations	XII	1 energies

> I leave it up to each astrologer to assess this. Heterodox or not, all this is very foreign to my notions of the planetary effect during the diurnal movement.[29]

Having read *Ceux qui nous guident*, with all its errors, as well as Lasson's unfortunate earlier publications, I felt no urge to test his claims directly, all the more since the first two groups of professionals that I studied – famous doctors and sportsmen[30] were not dealt with in Lasson's book. Choisnard's influence on me was more important.

All else aside, by moving the angular houses by one step, Lasson did stress the importance of planets that are positioned after their rising or culmination point and for this he deserves some credit. Nevertheless, I find it paradoxical – and even disturbing – that this idea should have germinated in the mind of one of the most bizarre and inconsistent astrologers I have encountered. What a place for the 'grain of gold' in astrology to find itself!

The only real merit of Choisnard, Krafft and Lasson is that they ensured a sort of continuity in astrological research. However, because of their errors, they have no right to the excuses we make for their glorious forebears. In the twentieth century, there are scientific methods that allow us to extract the famous 'grain of gold' from the layers of superstition. All that was needed was to discover the 'magic potion' to succeed. This magic potion is a very prosaic one indeed: it is a method of investigation worthy of its name, which makes work without errors possible, and produces convincing results. From this magic potion has come the 'Mars effect', and a whole series of similar observations which have caused a crack in the modern concepts of the universe for the astrological fact to slip through.

Epilogue:

FROM THE HARMONY OF THE SPHERES TO CHAOS

In the previous chapters, I have tried to show that neo-astrology has had many forerunners, from Babylonian times to the twentieth century. They are precursors in varying degrees and with disparate fortunes, but all have intuitively realized what constitutes the two main pillars of neo-astrology: the reality of planetary types and the power of the four celestial angles. Just as in astronomy, Copernicus had a predecessor by the name Aristarchos of Samos, who lived 1,800 years before him.

The facts have been established, and Science can no longer ignore my results. I have shown how they were verified by a reluctant and horrified scientific community. The Mars effect has overcome the cleverest traps that were placed in its path. As cold, impersonal and objective as the statistical method from which it is derived, neo-astrology emerges as a doctrine that is at the same time very new and very old, It is now clear that astrology must be reassessed in the light of recent discoveries. Scientists must reinstate the idea of astrology in their Universe, where there is no place at the moment for 'astrological waves'.

How can we reconcile the past and the present? We have an urgent need for a new paradigm to be able to understand the Universe. New? I would rather say lost, forgotten. Astrology's 'Aristarchoses of Samos' were numerous but inept. They did not know how to separate the wheat from the chaff and finally – almost – lost the wheat. Now that it has been rediscovered, assigned its true worth, and proved, astrologers have the duty to discard the chaff. In fact, like scientists, astrologers are confronted by the painful revision of their belief. It is not *one* but *two* revolutions that are taking place, although not on the same plane.

The first is an *interior* revolution, within astrology itself, a 'small' Copernican revolution. The results I present are often negative, which, I imagine, does not satisfy astrologers. The fact that statistical findings reject the multiplicity of horoscopic factors: zodiac, aspects, houses, transits, directions – and even the planets Mercury, Uranus, Neptune, Pluto and above all, the Sun – must indeed be frustrating for them. Unlike astrology, neo-astrology is extremely frugal. It entirely boils down to experimental proof of the influence on the personality of the five planets, Saturn, Jupiter, Mars, Venus and the Moon, depending on whether or not the planet is positioned at birth in the Gauquelin 'plus zones'. This is not much from an astrologer's point of view. Of course, there is always the possibility that some future researcher, more capable than I, will prove scientifically that there is more to astrology than I think. This possibility cannot be discarded. For the moment, however, this is not the case, and astrologers must admit that the distance between the horoscopic doctrine and neo-astrology is such that it presents a veritable revolution for this doctrine. As for them accepting this revolution, I realize that they will not do so without a fight. Nevertheless, astrologers still have one satisfaction: they now know that they have safeguarded the *essential*: the fact that planets exert an influence at birth has been, finally, rigorously, even parsimoniously, proved.

Of a completely different order of importance, is the second revolution, the one that really counts, the 'big' *external* one. This time, astrology is not shaken from within by decisive changes, but in its purified scientific form it is once more imposing itself upon Science. Shortly before his death, C. G. Jung – who was, incidentally, kept informed about my work through Hans Bender, professor of psychology at Freiburg University in Germany – intuitively perceived this possible revolution: 'The cultural Philistines believed until recently that astrology had been disposed of long since and was something that could safely be laughed at. But today, rising

From the Harmony of the Spheres to Chaos

out the social deeps, it knocks at the doors of the universities from which it was banished some three hundred years ago.'

Neo-astrology imposes a revision of ideas on the structure of the Universe and on the relationship between man and the cosmos. But, for the moment, does it provide a plausible scientific model to explain the planetary effects?

Let us, for example, take the effect of Mars on sportsmen. How does the planet act on the child at birth, and why is the child sensitive to it? The difficulties in answering this question are considerable – the scientific world believes them to be insurmountable. Nevertheless, it is essential to construct an explanatory model. Until such a model is found, a new theory cannot be presented, and the astrological Copernican revolution cannot be entirely completed. The Mars effect – and neo-astrology in general – needs to be integrated into current knowledge in order to be transformed from top to bottom. Without this happening, only a strange epiphenomenon remains, admittedly a disturbing anomaly for 'normal science', but nothing more. We must not deceive ourselves: this revolution – external to astrology – has only just begun. Two major hypotheses can be put forward to explain the planetary effects on a child: the 'imprint' theory and the 'midwife planet' theory.

The 'imprint' theory was well known by Renaissance occultist astrologers. It is the famous theory of planetary 'signatures', mentioned in the previous chapter, according to which at the moment of birth a planet puts its imprint on the soul of the child, thereby influencing its whole personality.

Although this theory remaind linked to the *hermetic* concept of affinities between the human soul and the cosmos, it is coherent. Even better, I have shown how far the notion of 'signatures' had fulfilled its promise, and how much my descriptions of planetary temperaments owe to it. But can we easily translate this *hermetic* concept into a *scientific* explanation? To talk of the 'Harmony of the World' is one thing. To prove the mechanics of the Mars effect, is another.

Can the 'imprint' theory be translated into 'physical' terms? On paper, undoubtedly. It is enough to accept that the planet adds something to the child at birth which was not included in the hereditary package. A child born when Mars is rising thereby has more energy than other people, and its chances of being successful in sport are increased. In this form, the 'imprint' theory is difficult to accept and both biologists and astronomers find it rather absurd. According to them, when a child is born it is completely formed, all its potentials having been inherited from its parents. How can we then accept that – *at that moment* – a planet affects the chromosomal structure of the child's cells, disrupts it and redistributes it to the point of giving a decisive orientation to its character?

I have mentioned that Ptolemy already perceived the main difficulty and maintained that it was the *conception* chart which should count, as it would be cast at the very moment when the 'chromosomal lottery' was taking place: Mars could thus affect (but how?) the chromosomal distribution at the precise moment when the sperm was penetrating the egg and impregnating it. This would seem to be a logical – if not plausible – way of understanding how Mars can exert a decisive influence on a child's future character.

Nevertheless, the Mars effect is considered from the moment of birth, which is, without doubt, too late. I have shown how Ptolemy coped with the difficulty by subtle reasoning. For him, although the time of conception does count, the time of birth counts even more because the planetary configurations which preside over conception are reproduced at birth. Unfortunately, Ptolemy did not prove this hypothesis, which is well thought out, although virtually unverifiable. All this shows that even in antiquity the 'imprint' theory was already causing extremely prickly problems as far as the matter of *physical* influence was concerned. Hence, the second hypothesis.

The 'midwife planet' theory also has its supporters. Paying tribute to Kepler and even Ptolemy, Choisnard explains it: 'We are born under a particular sky because we are so predisposed, already shaped by heredity and gestation.'[1] In other words, the planets set off labour when it is time, acting as 'midwife planets', and heredity is linked to this trigger action.

I have personally done a great deal of work on this hypothesis. A whole series of experiments led me to observe in 1966 what I have called 'planetary heredity'. And here is my main finding: if the father (or mother) is born with a planet (Venus, Mars, Jupiter, Saturn or the Moon) in one of the Gauquelin 'plus zones', the child has a tendency to be born with the same planet in the same zones.[2] Armed with this discovery, I defined the model of 'midwife planets' as follows:

> The foetus appears to be endowed with a 'planetary sensibility' that stimulates its entry into the world at a given moment in the daily course of this or that planet, rather than at some other time. This planetary sensibility seems to be of genetic origin, and the planet itself not to modify the organism of the newborn child. Instead, it seems to act as the 'trigger', the 'activator' in parturition, while its position in the sky simply reflects the psychological temperament of the child.[3]

The 'midwife planet' theory solves some of the difficulties arising from the 'imprint' theory. Moreover, with the observation of planetary heredity, it has found its first experimental justification. When, a while later, I noticed that the intensity of the planetary parent-child link appeared to vary with the effects of terrestrial magnetism, I really believed I was on the road to a 'physical' planetary explanation of the Gauquelin planetary effect.[4]

I realize today that my optimism was premature. Firstly because, fairly recently – in 1984 – I experienced difficulties in reproducing the first planetary heredity results, which raises doubt about the existence of this phenomenon,[5] but also because, even if this phenomenon is real, it only succeeds in creating another mystery.

In fact, if planets trigger off birth, they must affect, above all, the *beginning* of labour, rather than the *end*, that is, the time of birth. This makes the planet-trigger model very vulnerable when studied in relation to the instant of birth. We now know that the full-term foetus is the cause of the beginning of the delivery, provoking contractions in the maternal uterus through a complex hormonal mechanism. But the amount of time that passes between the beginning of labour and the actual birth is not fixed. The length of labour depends on numerous factors independent of the planets: the weight of the foetus, the age and the physical constitution of the mother, etc.

This objection has not eluded me. In response, I have collected several thousand times corresponding to the beginning of labour in maternity records. I then submitted this data to the same hypothesis of planetary heredity as for the time of birth (I shall omit here the technical details). The results were not convincing. It is of course true that the time of the start of labour is not noted as precisely as the time of birth. Nevertheless, the evidence clearly indicates that the time of birth remains the favoured instant for the detection of planetary effects, which remains a sort of biological 'scandal' in respect of the phenomenon of birth.[6]

Another prickly question is that of induced births. These are more and more frequent. In January 1989, I was in Miami when I came across an article in the local paper giving the number of births by Caesarean section in the town hospitals in 1988. The average was around 50 per cent. (The world average is lower, but is rapidly growing. The day may well come when vaginal delivery will become a sort of medical incongruity.) In all these cases, it is the doctor who decides the time of birth. The child no longer has the leisure to 'choose' when it is time to come into the world according to the state of the sky, and in compatibility with its heredity.

In fact, I have shown that planetary heredity disappears at the birth of a child after any surgical intervention.[7] From the angle of the 'midwife planet' theory, this was foreseeable: in the case of surgical intervention, the doctor decides on the sky of the child's birth, and the planets no longer have the possibility of playing their triggering role. If its birth has been induced, or is in any way not natural, the child will carry what could be called a *false planetary identity card*. All of which would appear to be prejudicial to the future of neo-astrology as an instrument of diagnosing temperament and traits of character.

On the other hand, the principle of artificial delivery has an advantage. It allows us to compare the respective merit of the 'imprint' theory and of the 'midwife planet' theory from experience. Once more, the Mars effect on sports champions will serve as a test.

From the Harmony of the Spheres to Chaos

At the time, now long ago, of my discovery of the Mars effect, births were, so to speak, quite natural.

However, let us suppose that on the contrary I select from the new generation of champions *only* those born by Caesarean or after an artificially induced labour. If the Mars effect disappears in this new group, the 'midwife planet' theory will find itself strengthened. If it remains, we will no doubt need to return to the 'imprint' theory. This verification is under way. Its results will be important whatever they are, but they will be far from resolving everything. The 'imprint' and the 'midwife planet' theories have so shaken up both astrophysicists and biologists that they have opted for out-of-hand dismissal: for them they amount to nothing but hot air: they are theories created in the quicksand of physical impossibilities. I fully realize the extent to which even the 'midwife planet' theory is a fragile model.

In his book *Forget Your Sun-Sign*, Anthony Standen describes accurately, from the viewpoint of orthodox science, the gulf that today separates my results from a 'rational' explanation:

> We have seen how little we receive from the planets. Utterly negligible gravitation, hardly anything perceptive, except for those blasts of radio noise from Jupiter in a rhythm of not quite ten hours. And yet, to explain Gauquelin, the planets, out to Saturn, must be sending us some kind of influence that goes through the walls of the building where the delivery is taking place. And also, since there is a slight effect on the opposite side of the earth, it must go through the earth, or else go round it.
>
> Why should it have an effect only at the moment of birth? This 'radiation' or 'influence' or whatever you call it is coming to us from the planets all the time, presumably. If it has any effect on the baby's first breath, does it not also affect the baby's second breath, and indeed, all subsequent breaths? And the breaths of those attending the delivery? Both on the when-the-foetus-is ready theory and on the baby's-first-breath theory, is equally inexplicable.
>
> Does it affect *all* mankind? Or only those born in well-equipped hospitals in Western Europe? Does it affect Africa? South America? Australia? Has it been this way since prehistoric times? Did it affect

Cro-Magnon man? Neanderthal man? All hominids? Australopithecus? How far down in the biological scale does it go?

And finally, who on earth can believe in the extraordinary spotty way in which this 'influence' is said to act? [the Gauquelin 'plus zones'] ... At any position on the Earth's surface, the influence of any of these planets is two hours on, four hours off, then two hours on again ... Can anyone believe that?[8]

I am consoled by the thought that Copernicus himself was unable to supply well-founded physical proof of his theory. The proof was provided only later, thanks to the work of his successors. Copernicus himself only instigated the Copernican revolution. It is the same with neo-astrology. Its great value is that it poses new questions to science. This does not mean that it is in the position of answering them. The Mars effect is a challenge. It poses a problem, and when it is resolved, a new revolution of ideas will have been accomplished. But from the moment they accept the reality of Mars effect, researchers can no longer think of the world, or their relation to it, in the same way as before.

For Standen, the extreme scepticism shown towards me by scientists is entirely justified. But he immediately adds:

> They would be greatly to be blamed if they did nothing about Gauquelin! What is science for? To find out about the world we live in. Is it this kind of a world, or that kind? Or come other kind? Does it follow regularities, or 'laws', and if so, what are these laws? If anyone is imbued with a passionate desire to find out about the world we live in – and any scientist worth the name ought to be driven by such a desire – he should be inspired to a tremendous effort by the claims of Gauquelin. He cannot believe them, but then he should have an utter determination to find out for certain whether they are true or not. Because if they are true, then we *must not* ignore them, no matter how extravagant they appear to us to be.[8]

Today, a number of researchers have worked on the Gauquelin effect and proposed some ingenious explanations. The chief lecturer in astronomy at the Plymouth Polytechnic Institute, Percy Seymour, has just revealed his theory in *Astrology: The Evidence of Science*,[9] in which he explains my observations by linking the planetary effects with Earth's magnetism. His work has, of course, stirred up indignation among his astronomical colleagues. For my part, however, I hail Seymour's courage and I am pleased that his work has attracted the media's attention.[10]

In Germany, two researchers, Arno Müller[11] and Suitbert Ertel,[12] both psychologists and university professors but working independently of each other, have thought a good deal about my observations and published their interpretations of them.

Seymour, Müller and Ertel all remain firmly attached to the scientific model. Others have considered it necessary to go further. Peter Roberts, a physicist and visiting professor at the City University of London, has just published *The Message of Astrology*.[13] In explaining the Gauquelin effect, Roberts wonders if Seymour's theory goes far enough: 'I argue in my book,' he says, 'that you can't explain astrology using ordinary physics alone. You've got to move into the paranormal to do it.'[14] Roberts agrees with the ideas of his late friend, the astrologer John Addey, that the planetary effects are above all a harmonic resultant without a real physical substratum. A quasi-Pythagorean concept, which would not have been repudiated by Kepler, with his 'Harmony of the Spheres'.

But who will be the Einstein who calculates the 'astrological waves' and their laws? No one yet knows. Nor is it known when the calculations will be achieved. Lord Keynes called Newton 'the last magician'. But why should he be the last? It is true, however, that only another 'magician' of that calibre will be able to discover the secret of an enigma posed by the priest-astrologers of Babylonia. Such a magician will have to account for both the alarming existence of planetary symbolism which goes back to more than 4,000 years,[15] and for the Babylonian omen linking the birth of a child when Mars is rising with a 'hot temper' (because my statistical experiments have proved this omen to be true). It would be wrong to explain the Babylonian intuition by assuming that they connected the planet Mars with war simply because of its red colour, which recalls the blood of battlefields: my findings show that military leaders are *actually* born at the moment of the planet's strong intensity.

*

There is only one way to achieve understanding: to think in *another* way. For several years now, physicists have done this. They already think about physics in another way and do not hesitate to link it to some oriental religious concepts. Fritjof Capra, in his *The Tao of Physics*,[16] is a case in point. He states: 'The mechanistic concept of the world of classical physics ... turns out to be incapable of accounting for physical phenomena in the domain of infra-atomics.'[17] Pierre Thuillier comments on this:

> This is why he hopes that westerners will study oriental thought and will acquire a new vision of nature. For example, according to Capra, Taoists are right in thinking that the phenomena are underlined by a continuous cosmic flux. This dynamic concept, he says, accounts for the structure of matter, which *dances* and *vibrates* according to the rhythm determined by molecular, atomic and nuclear structures. In a general way, the mental set of western physics is too rigid. The 'rational, masculine and aggressive' *yang* attitude needs to be complemented by the feminine *yin* attitude, spiritually concerned and sensitive to the harmony of the world.[18]

The cosmic dance of Shiva – so wonderfully represented in oriental sculpture – can be linked to the *harmonia* of western tradition, from Pythagoras to Kepler. For neo-astrology, the link may be through Tao.

Recently, in his work, *Chaos: Making a New Science*,[19] James Gleick has perhaps revealed yet another way of coming to neo-astrology's aid. Chaos represents the world in a completely different way. Whereas science has until now searched for order in the disorder of things, Gleick tells the story of researchers who, on the contrary, have seen in disorder the key to many phenomena previously inexplicable. Purely mathematical in origin, *chaos* is a doctrine that leads to something concrete. In the words of Douglas Hofstadter, 'It turns out that an eerie type of chaos can lurk just behind a façade of order – and yet, deep inside the chaos lurks an even eerier type of order.'[20]

Here is a definition evocative of the chaotic diversity of astrology, where, searching hard I have nevertheless observed some sort of

From the Harmony of the Spheres to Chaos

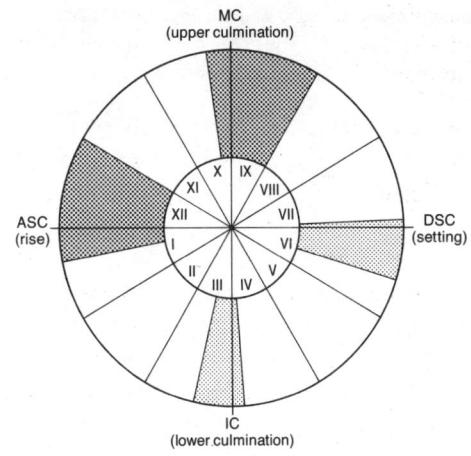

Figure 13: (top) Tibetan Mandala:
A Mandala is a figure which helps in meditation and communion with the Cosmos.
(bottom) Planetary effect in the Gauquelin 'plus zones':
The similarity of the diagrams (both are in the shape of the cross) is astonishing. Has it also a deeper meaning?

order. I do not know if the Mars effect can be explained through the 'fractal mathematics' described by Gleick, but there is reason to hope. Thus, from the Harmony of Spheres to chaos – after a long detour – astrology, purified, understood and accepted for itself, will at last find its place among the great laws of Nature, as the first law.

At the end of the twentieth century, two dreams must become reality: to go to the planets, but also to know what the planets 'do to us', so that as *The Emerald Table*[21] says, 'the miracle of unity may be perpetuated'.

NOTES

Preface: From Cosmic Clocks to Neo-Astrology

1 Frank A. Brown, preface to *The Cosmic Clocks*, Michel Gauquelin, Granada Publishing (London 1980), p. 14
2 Michel Gauquelin, *Cosmic Influences on Human Behavior*, Futura (London 1976); first published in the USA by Stein and Day, New York, in 1973
3 Michel Gauquelin, *The Truth About Astrology*, Blackwell (Oxford 1983), p. 179

Lifting the Curtain: Astrology as Universal Law

1 Lynn Thorndike, 'The True Place of Astrology in the History of Science', presented at the annual meeting of the History of Science Society on 30 December 1954
2 Herbert Dingle, quoted by Thorndike in 'The True Place of Astrology', p. 2
3 Thorndike, 'The True Place of Astrology'
4 Mircea Eliade, *The Sacred and the Profane*, Harcourt Brace Jovanovich (Orlando 1968), pp. 117–18
5 Franz Boll, *Storia dell'astrologia*, Lateza (Rome 1979), p. 16
6 Ernest Zinner, *The Stars Above Us*, Allen & Unwin (London 1957), p. 6
7 Maurice Lambert, 'La lune chez les Sumériens', *La lune, mythes et rites*, Seuil (Paris 1962), p. 75
8 Ibid., p. 84
9 Ibid., p. 85

10 Eliade, *The Sacred and the Profane*, p. 156
11 Lambert, 'La lune chez les Sumériens', p. 88
12 Ibid., p. 84
13 Zinner, *The Stars above Us*, p. 10
14 Ibid.
15 Ibid., p. 11

ACT ONE: CAST OF CHARACTERS
2 The Gauquelin Results

1 For further details see, for example, Michel Gauquelin, *The Truth about Astrology*, Blackwell (Oxford 1983); *Written in the Stars*, Aquarian Press (Wellingborough 1988)
2 I have actually been to Iraq, visited Ur and climbed the steps of the tower to the top. Michel Gauquelin, 'Pilgrimage to Sumer' in *Cosmic Influences on Human Behavior*, Aurora Press (Santa Fe 1985), pp. 259–62
3 Gauquelin, *Written in the Stars*, Appendix I, pp. 199–202
4 Michel Gauquelin, *L'influence des astres*, Le Dauphin (Paris 1955), Part II, Chapters 2 and 3; *Written in the Stars*
5 Michel Gauquelin, *Les hommes et les astres*, Denoël (Paris 1960); *Written in the Stars*
6 Gauquelin, *L'influence des astres*, pp. 82–3
7 Michel and Françoise Gauquelin, *Psychological Monographs*, 4 volumes, LERRCP (Paris 1974–7)
8 Astronomically, it is not strictly the correct way of expressing this, but it is an approximation close enough for my needs here. (For more details see Gauquelin, *Written in the Stars*, Appendix I
9 Michel Gauquelin, *The Spheres of Destiny*, Dent/Corgi (London 1981); *Cosmic Influences on Human Behavior*

3 Science and the Mars Effect

1 Thomas Kuhn, *The Copernican Revolution*, Harvard University Press (Cambridge, Mass., 1957), p. 75
2 George Abell, Foreword to Michel Gauquelin's *Dreams and Illusions of Astrology*, Prometheus (New York 1979)

Notes

3 Thomas Kuhn, *The Structure of the Scientific Revolutions*, Chicago University Press (Chicago 1962)

4 Max Plank, *Scientific Autobiography and Other Papers* (New York, 1949), pp. 33–4

5 Paul Feyerabend, *Against Method*, New Left Books (London 1975)

6 'Objections to Astrology', a statement by 192 leading scientists, in *The Humanist*, 35, no. 5 (September/October 1975)

7 Ibid.

8 Arthur Mather, 'Response to Reviews of Dean and Mather (1977)', in *Zetetic Scholar*, 3 and 4 (1979), pp. 94–6

9 Patrick Curry, 'Research on the "Mars Effect"', *Zetetic Scholar*, 9 (1982); Michel Gauquelin, 'Science and Proof', in *The Truth About Astrology*, Blackwell (London 1983), pp. 97–114

10 Michel Gauquelin, *L'influence des astres*, Le Dauphin (Paris 1955)

11 Karl Popper, *The Logic of Scientific Discovery*, Hutchinson (London 1959)

12 Comité belge pour l'étude des phénomènes réputés paranormaux (Comité Para): 'Considérations critiques sur une recherche faite par M. M. Gauquelin dans le domaine des influences planétaires', in *Nouvelles Brèves*, 43 (1976), pp. 327–43

13 Hans Eysenck, 'Planets, Stars and Personality', in *New Behavior* (1975), pp. 246–9

14 Michel and Françoise Gauquelin, 'The Zelen Test of the Mars Effect', in *The Humanist* (November/December 1977), pp. 30–5

15 Marvin Zelen, Paul Kurtz and George Abell, 'Is There a Mars Effect?', in *The Humanist* (November/December 1977), pp. 36–7

16 Dennis Rawlins, 'sTarbaby', in *Fate* (October 1981), pp. 67–98; Richard Kamman, 'The True Disbelievers: Mars Effect Drives Skeptics to Irrationality', in *Zetetic Scholar*, 10 (1982)

17 T. J. Pinch and H. M. Collins, 'Private Science and Public Knowledge: The CSICOP and its Use of Literature' in *Social Studies of Science*, 14 (1984), pp. 521–46

18 Marcello Truzzi, 'Introduction to 'Research on the Mars Effect"', in *Zetetic Scholar*, 9 (1982)

19 Henry Krips, 'Astrology – Fad, Fiction or Forecast?', in *Erkenntnis*, 14 (1979), p. 373
20 George Abell, Paul Kurtz and Marvin Zelen, 'The Abell-Kurtz-Zelen "Mars Effect" Experiments: A Reappraisal', in *The Skeptical Inquirer* (Spring 1983), pp. 77–82
21 Suitbert Ertel, 'Raising the Hurdle for the Athletes 'Mars Effect: Association co-varies with Eminence', in *Journal of Scientific Exploration*, 2 (1988), pp. 53–82; and 'Gauquelins Planetenhypothese: Stein des Anstosses oder Prüfstein der Vernunft', in *Psychologische Rundschau*, 39 (1988), pp. 179–90
22 Thomas Kuhn, *The Copernican Revolution*, p. 75

First Interlude: In Search of a Lost Paradigm

1 Thomas Kuhn, *The Copernican Revolution*, Harvard University Press (Cambridge, Mass., 1957), p. 4
2 George Sarton, *A History of Science*, Vol. 2, Cambridge University Press (Cambridge 1952), p. 57
3 Ibid. pp. 56–7
4 Kuhn, *The Copernican Revolution*, p. 74
5 Paul Thagard, 'Why Astrology is a Pseudo-Science', in *Introductory Reading in the Philosophy of Science*, Klemke, Hollinger & Kine eds. (1988), pp. 16–75

ACT TWO: THE BABYLONIANS

4 On the Way to the Horoscope

1 B. L. Van der Waerden, *Science Awakening*, Vol. 2, Oxford University Press (New York 1970)
2 Otto Neugebauer, *The Exact Sciences in Antiquity*, Brown University Press (Providence 1957), p. 53
3 Ibid. p. 58
4 Ibid. p. 59
5 Van der Waerden, *Science Awakening*, p. 58
6 Ibid., p. 98

Notes

7 Neugebauer, *The Exact Sciences in Antiquity*, p. 98
8 Van der Waerden, *Science Awakening*, p. 77
9 Ibid., pp. 77–8
10 Van der Waerden, 'History of the Zodiac', in *Archiv für Orientforschung*, 16, 2 (1953), p. 220
11 Ibid.
12 Ibid.
13 Van der Waerden, *Science Awakening*, p. 128.

5 An Early 'Grain of Gold'?

1 Michel Gauquelin, *L'influence des astres*, Le Dauphin (Paris 1955)
2 A. Sachs, 'Babylonian Horoscopes', in *Journal of Cuneiform Studies*, VI, no. 2 (1952), pp. 49–75. All the following translations (see pp. 58–62) from Babylonian tablets are extracted from this article.
3 Ibid. p. 51
4 Ibid. p. 52
5 Otto Neugebauer, *The Exact Sciences in Antiquity*, Brown University Press (Providence 1957)
6 Sachs, 'Babylonian Horoscopes', p. 52
7 Ibid.
8 Ibid., p. 60
9 Ibid., p. 65
10 Ibid., p. 75
11 B. L. Van der Waerden, *Science Awakening*, Vol. 2, Oxford University Press (New York 1970), p. 78
12 Sachs, 'Babylonian Horoscopes', p. 74

ACT THREE: GREEK ASTROLOGY

6 The Four Pillars of the Sky

1 A. Sachs, 'Babylonian Horoscopes', *Journal of Cuneiform Studies*, VI, no. 2 (1952), p. 53

2 A. Bouché-Leclercq, *L'astrologie grecque*, Leroux (Paris 1899)
3 Franz Boll, *Storia dell'astrologia*, Laterza (Rome 1979)
4 Franz Cumont, *Astrology and Religion Among the Greeks and Romans*, Dover (New York, 1960), p. 98
5 Fr. H. Cramer, *Astrology in Roman Law and Politics*, The American Philosophical Society, (Philadelphia 1954)
6 Otto Neugebauer and H. B. Van Hoesen, *Greek Horoscopes*, The American Philosophical Society (Philadelphia 1959)
7 Manilius, *Astronomicon*, Harvard University Press (Cambridge, Mass., 1977)
8 Ptolemy, *Tetrabiblos*, translated by F. E. Robbins, Harvard University Press (Cambridge, Mass., 1956)
9 Firmicus, *Mathesis*, translated by J. R. Bram, Noyes Press (Park Ridge 1975)
10 Arthur Koestler, *The Sleepwalkers*, Penguin (London 1986), p. 29
11 Ibid., pp. 31–2
12 Louis Rougier, *La Religion astrale de pythagoriciens*, P.U.F. (Paris 1959), p. 58
13 Ibid., p. 94
14 Ptolemy, *Anthol. Palal.* ix, p. 577, quoted by Cumont, op. cit., p. 81
15 Cumont, *Astrology and Religion Among the Greeks and Romans*, p. 40
16 Neugebauer and Van Hoesen, *Greek Horoscopes*, p. 3
17 Ibid., figures 9 and 20
18 Manilius, *Astronomicon*, pp. 145–7
19 Ptolemy, *Tetrabiblos*, I, 24, p. 117
20 Quoted by A. Bouché-Leclercq in *L'astrologie grecque*
21 Manilius, *Astronomicon*, p. 151
22 Ptolemy, *Tetrabiblos*, p. 273
23 Ibid.
24 Ibid.
25 J. D. North, *Horoscopes and History*, The Warburg Institute (London 1986), p. 6
26 Ibid., p. 7

7 Astral Psychology

1 Franz Cumont, *Astrology and Religion Among the Greeks and Romans*, Dover (New York 1960), p. 27
2 Ibid.
3 Ibid.
4 Ibid.
5 J. C. Eade, *The Forgotten Sky*, Oxford University Press (New York 1984), p. 66
6 Hippocrates, *Treatise on Humours*
7 Simon Kemp, 'Personality in Ancient Astrology', in *New Ideas in Psychology*, 6, 5 (1988), pp. 267–72
8 Ibid., p. 267
9 Michel Gauquelin, *La Cosmopsychologie*, Retz (Paris 1974), Appendix; *La Tétrabible de Ptolémée*, 'Les qualités de l'Ame', pp. 231–5
10 Ptolemy, *Tetrabiblos*, translated by F. E. Robbins, Harvard University Press (Cambridge, Mass., 1956), III, 13, 'Of the Quality of the Soul'
11 Firmicus, *Mathesis*, translated by J. R. Bram, Noyes Press (Park Ridge 1975), Chapter XIX, 'The Ruler of the Chart', p. 156
12 Ptolemy, *Tetrabiblos*, p. 341
13 Firmicus, *Mathesis*, p. 156
14 Otto Neugebauer and H. B. Van Hoesen, *Greek Horoscopes*, The American Philosophical Society (Philadelphia 1959), p. 156
15 A. Bouché-Leclercq, *L'astrologie grecque*, Leroux (Paris 1899)
16 Neugebauer and Van Hoesen, *Greek Horoscopes*, p. 176
17 Ibid., plate 12, no. 76
18 Vettius Valens, quoted by Neugebauer and Van Hoesen, *Greek Horoscopes*, p. 90
19 Marguerite Yourcenar, *Les mémoires d'Hadrien*, Plon (Paris 1958), p. 1

Second Interlude: Kepler: Astronomer, Astrologer

1 Jean Seznec, *The Survival of the Pagan Gods*, Harper & Row (New York 1961), p. 2

2 Ibid., p. 3
3 Gérard Simon, *Képler: astronome, astrologue*, Gallimard (Paris 1977), p. 444
4 Arthur Koestler, *The Sleepwalkers*, Penguin (London 1986), p. 251
5 Johannes Kepler, *Tertius Interveniens*, Frankfurt, 1610
6 Wolfgang Pauli, *The Influence of Archetypal Ideas on Kepler's Theories*, Routledge & Kegan Paul (London 1955), pp. 180, 182
7 Johannes Kepler, *Harmonices Mundi*, Book IV (Linz 1619)
8 Johannes Kepler, *De Stella Nova*, Capt. 28 (Prague – Frankfurt 1606)
9 C. G. Jung, *Synchronicity, an Acausal Connecting Principle*, Routledge & Kegan Paul (London 1955), p. 112
10 Simon, *Képler: astronome, astrologue*, p. 120
11 Johannes Kepler, *Horoscope de Wallenstein*, Opera Omnia, I, p. 387
12 Simon, *Képler: astronome, astrologue*, p. 121
13 Johannes Kepler, quoted by Simon in *Képler: astrologue, astronome*, p. 127
14 Simon, *Képler: astronome, astrologue*, pp. 221-2
15 Kepler, *De Stella Nova*, Capt. 10, quoted by Simon in *Képler: astronome, astrologue*, p. 222
16 Kepler, *Harmonices Mundi*
17 Michel Gauquelin, *The Truth About Astrology*, Chapter 8, 'Midwife Planets', Blackwell (London 1983)
18 Johannes Kepler's letters to Maestlin (1598)
19 Michel Gauquelin, *Planetary Heredity*, ACS Publications (San Diego 1988), Chapter 8, 'Astrology and Heredity'
20 Ptolemy, *Tetrabiblos*, III, 1, pp. 225-7
21 Kepler, quoted by Simon in *Képler: astronome, astrologue*, p. 33

ACT FOUR: THE RENAISSANCE

8 The Last Magicians

1 Petrarch, quoted by Eugenio Garin, in *Astrology in the Renaissance*, Routledge & Kegan Paul (London 1982), p. 8

Notes

2 Jean Seznec, *The Survival of Pagan Gods*, Harper & Row (New York 1961), p. 173
3 Wayne Shumaker, *The Occult Sciences in the Renaissance*, University of California Press (Los Angeles 1972), p. 21
4 Ibid.
5 Ibid.
6 Ibid., pp. 21–2.
7 Pico della Mirandola, quoted by Garin in *Astrology in the Renaissance*, p. 80
8 Guy Bechtel, *Paracelse*, C.A.L. (Paris 1970), p. 155
9 Ibid.
10 Ibid., p. 156
11 Paracelsus, *Paragranum*, P.U.F., Galien collection (Paris 1968), pp. 47–8
12 Ibid., pp. 57, 73
13 Ibid., p. 63
14 Shumaker, *The Occult Sciences in the Renaissance*, p. 38
15 Henri Selva, *La théorie des déterminations astrologiques de Morin de Villefranche*, Bodin (Paris no date), pp. 210–11
16 Shumaker, *The Occult Sciences in the Renaissance*, p. 38
17 Ibid., p. 41
18 Ibid.
19 Wilhelm Knappich, *Histoire de l'astrologie*, LeBaud (Paris 1988), pp. 188, 189
20 Henri Selva, *La domification, ou construction du thème céleste en astrologie*, Vigot (Paris 1917)
21 Françoise and Michel Gauquelin, *Méthodes pour étudier la répartition des astres dans le mouvement diurne*, LERRCP (Paris 1957)
22 Michel Gauquelin, *Written in the Stars*, Appendix 1: 'Short Guide to Methods', Aquarian Press (Wellingborough, 1988), pp. 197–217
23 Lynn Thorndike, *History of Magic and Experimental Sciences*, 8 volumes, Chapter 39, 'Sir Isaac Newton', Columbia University Press (New York 1929–58), p. 589
24 W. Wightman, *Science in a Renaissance Society*, Hutchinson (London 1972), p. 142

25 Pierre Thuillier, *Les savoirs ventriloques*, Seuil (Paris 1983), p. 83
26 Ibid.
27 Ibid.
28 Lynn Thorndike, *The True Place of Astrology in the History of Science*, paper presented at the annual meeting of the History of Science Society, on 30 December 1954

9 Saturn and Melancholy

1 Johnstone Parr, *Tamburlaine's Malady and Other Essays on Astrology in Elizabethan Drama*, University of Alabama Press (Kingsport 1953), p. 22
2 Jean Seznec, *The Survival of the Pagan Gods*, Harper & Row (New York 1961), pp. 60–1
3 Marsilio Ficino, *Epistolae* (Florence 1495), quoted by Jean Seznec in *The Survival of the Pagan Gods*, p. 61
4 J. C. Eade, *The Forgotten Sky*, Oxford University Press (New York 1984), p. 52
5 Middleton, quoted by Eade in *The Forgotten Sky*, p. 54
6 Robert Burton, quoted by Eade in *The Forgotten Sky*, p. 91
7 Middleton, quoted by Eade, Ibid.
8 Wayne Shumaker, *The Occult Sciences in the Renaissance*, University of California (Los Angeles 1972), p. 5
9 R. Klibansky, E. Panofsky and F. Saxl, *Saturn and Melancholy*, Nelson (London 1964)
10 Frances Yates, *The Occult Philosophy in the Elizabethan Age*, Routledge & Kegan Paul (London 1979), p. 50
11 Ibid., p. 51
12 Parr, *Tamburlaine's Malady*, p. 40. The following quotes from Alchabitius, Ferrier, Agrippa, and Lilly are quoted from Parr's work
13 Michel Gauquelin, *Your Personality and the Planets*, Stein & Day (New York 1984), also as *Sphere of Destiny*, Corgi (London 1981)
14 Yates, *The Occult Philosophy*, p. 51

Notes

15 Michel Gauquelin, *L'influence des astres*, Le Dauphin (Paris 1955); *Written in the Stars*, Aquarian Press (Wellingborough 1988)
16 Yates, *The Occult Philosophy*, p. 52
17 Ibid., p. 52
18 Ibid., p. 54
19 Rudolf and Margot Wittkower, *Born Under Saturn: The Character and Conduct of Artists: a Documented History from Antiquity to the French Revolution*, Preface, Norton (New York 1963), pp. XXIV, and 63

10 Children of the Planets

1 Jean Seznec, *The Survival of the Pagan Gods*, Harper & Row (New York 1961), pp. 70–1
2 Ibid., p. 190
3 Ibid. p. 72
4 Wayne Shumaker, *The Occult Sciences in the Renaissance*, University of California (Los Angeles 1972), p. 5
5 This extract and those that follow (pp. 129–131) are by Johnstone Parr, *Tamburlaine's Malady and Other Essays on Astrology in Elizabethan Drama*, University of Alabama Press (Kingsport 1953), pp. 42–5 and pp. 46–8
6 Ibid., p. 67
7 Michel Gauquelin, *Cosmic Influences on Human Behavior*, Futura (London 1976); *Spheres of Destiny*, Corgi (London 1981)
8 Parr, *Tamburlaine's Malady*, Chapter 4: 'Astrology Motivates a Comedy', pp. 38–49
9 Ibid., p. 39
10 Ibid., pp. 39–43
11 Quoted by Seznec in *The Survival of the Pagan Gods*, p. 80
12 Gauquelin, *Cosmic Influences on Human Behavior*, pp. 218–25
13 Parr, in this chapter, also analyses these descriptions taken from Ptolemy and Firmicus
14 Michel and Françoise Gauquelin, *Psychological Monographs*, 4 volumes, LERRCP (Paris 1973–7)

15 Michel Gauquelin, 'Planetary Influences: An Empirical Study of the Accuracy of "Ancient" Astrologers "Key Words"' in *Correlation* (1982), 2, 2, pp. 4–11

ACT FIVE: THE TWENTIETH CENTURY

11   The Trojan Horse

1 Mark Graubard, *Astrology and Alchemy: Two Fossil Sciences*, Figure 20; 'The Rise and Fall of Astrology', Philosophical Library (New York 1953)
2 A. Bouché-Leclercq, *L'astrology grecque*, Leroux (Paris 1899)
3 Thomas Kuhn, *The Copernican Revolution*, Chapter 1, Harvard University Press (Cambridge, Mass., 1957)
4 Adolphe Quételet, *Essai de physique sociale* (Paris 1835), Vol. I, pp. 102–4
5 G. Allport and H. Odbert, 'Trait-names: A Psycho-lexical Study', in *Psychological Monographs*, 47 (1936)
6 W. Sheldon, *Les variétés de tempérament*, P.U.F. (Paris, 1950)
7 Hans Eysenck, *The Structure of Human Personality*, Methuen (London 1970)
8 Carl Sagan, *Broca's Brain*, Random House (New York 1979)
9 S. J. Gould, *The Mismeasure of Man*, Norton (New York 1981)
10 Paul Choisnard, *Le Calcul des probabilités appliqué à l'astrologie*; Chacornac (Paris 1914)

12   Unfortunate Forerunners

1 Madame du Hausset, in *Le roman de l'histoire*, Horizon de France (Paris)
2 Paul Choisnard, *Langage astral*, Chacornac (Paris 1902); 6th edition, Ed. Traditionnelles (Paris 1963)
3 Ibid., pp. 8–9
4 Ibid.
5 Ibid.
6 Ibid.

Notes

7 Paul Choisnard, *Preuves et bases de l'astrologie scientifique*, Charcornac (Paris 1921)
8 Michel Gauquelin, *L'influence des astres*, Part I, Le Dauphin (Paris 1955), 'Critique des Astrologues', Choisnard, pp. 26–37
9 Michel Gauquelin, *Written in the Stars*, Appendix II: 'The Critique of Choisnard', Aquarian Press (Wellingborough 1988), pp. 235–9
10 Choisnard, *Langage astral*, p. 136
11 Ibid., p. 114
12 Paul Choisnard, *Essai de psychologie astrale*, Alcan (Paris 1925), pp. 157–65
13 Paul Choisnard, *La Loi d'hérédité astrale*, Chacornac (Paris 1919)
14 Choisnard, *Essai de psychologie astrale*, p. 20
15 Michel Gauquelin, *Planetary Heredity*, 'Astrology and Heredity', ACS Publications (San Diego 1988), pp. 41–6
16 Choisnard, *Langage astral*, p. 208
17 Karl Ernst Krafft, *Traité d'astrobiologie*, pp. 1 and 12–13, Legrand (Paris 1939)
18 Gauquelin, *L'influence des astres*, pp. 38–57; *Written in the Stars*, Appendix II, Aquarian Press (Wellingborough 1988), pp. 240–5
19 Ellic Howe, *Le monde étrange des astrologues*, Laffont (Paris 1969)
20 Léon Lasson, *Astrologie mondiale: la loi des grands événements historiques: quinze ans de paix sur l'Europe*, Demain (Bruxelles 1938)
21 Léon Lasson, *A la recherche des planètes transplutoniennes*, Claude Depaire (Neuilly-sur-Marne 1954)
22 Léon Lasson, *Ceux qui nous guident*, Debresse (Paris 1946)
23 Jean Hiéroz, *Les Cahiers Astrologiques*, 6 and 8 (1946)
24 Gauquelin, *L'influence des astres*, pp. 197–8
25 Michel Gauquelin, 'Influence des astres et astrologie' in *Les Cahiers Astrologiques*, 62 (1956), pp. 117–22
26 Several authors, 'Étude comparative de deux séries d'observations' in *Les Cahiers Astrologiques* (Sept./Oct. 1971)

27 Geoffrey Dean et al., *Recent Advances in Natal Astrology*, Astrologic (1977), p. 381
28 Léon Lasson, *Traité d'astrologie moderne*, Claude Depaire (Neuilly-sur-Marne 1954), p. 52
29 Gauquelin, *Written in the Stars*, pp. 248–9
30 Gauquelin, *L'influence des astres*, Part II, chapters 2, 3 and 4; *Written in the Stars*, chapters 3–6

Epilogue: From the Harmony of the Spheres to Chaos

1 Paul Choisnard, *Essai de psychologie astrale*, Alcan (Paris 1925), p. 20
2 Michel Gauquelin, *Planetary Heredity*, ACS Publications (San Diego 1988)
3 Michel Gauquelin, *The Truth About Astrology*, Blackwell (Oxford 1983), p. 146
4 Michel Gauquelin, 'A Possible Hereditary Effect on Time of Birth in Relation to the Diurnal Movement of the Moon and the Nearest Planets; its Relationship with Geomagnetic Activity', in *International Journal of Biometeorology*, 11 (1967), p. 341
5 Michel Gauquelin, 'Planetary Heredity, a Reappraisal on Fifty Thousand Subjects', *New Birth Data Series*, volume 2, LERRCP (Paris 1984)
6 Gauquelin, *Planetary Heredity*, Chapter VII: 'The Onset of Labor', pp. 37–9
7 Ibid., pp. 24–9
8 Anthony Standen, *Forget Your Sun-Sign*, Legacy (Baton Rouge 1977), pp. 103 and 106
9 Percy Seymour, *Astrology: The Evidence of Science*, Penguin Books (London 1990)
10 Dava Sobel, 'Dr Zodiac', *Omni* (December 1989), pp. 60–72
11 Arno Müller, 'Planetary Influences on Human Behavior ("Gauquelin Effect"): Too Absurd for a Scientific Explanation?' in *Journal of Scientific Exploration* (1990), 4, pp. 85–104
12 Suitbert Ertel, 'Raising the Hurdle for the Athletes' Mars Effect:

Association co-varies with Eminence', in *Journal of Scientific Exploration* (1988), 2, pp. 53–82
13 Peter Roberts, *The Message of Astrology*, Aquarian Press (1990 Wellingborough)
14 Peter Roberts, quoted in *Omni* (December 1989), p. 72
15 Françoise Gauquelin, *Astrological Symbolism and the Character Trait Method* (Foreword by Michel Gauquelin), Series D, Volume VII, LERRCP (Paris 1980)
16 Fritjof Capra, *The Tao of Physics*, Random House (New York 1985)
17 Pierre Thuillier, *Les savoirs ventriloques*, Sevil (Paris 1983), p. 118
18 Ibid. p. 119
19 James Gleick, *Chaos: Making a New Science*, Penguin Books, (London 1987)
20 Douglas Hofstadter, quoted by Gleick in *Chaos* (back cover)
21 Text attributed to the legendary Hermes Trismegistus (*c.* 4 B.C.) and part of the hermetic tradition: 'As above so below [. . .] and the miracle of unity may be perpetuated'.

ARKANA – NEW-AGE BOOKS FOR MIND, BODY AND SPIRIT

A selection of titles

With over 200 titles currently in print, Arkana is the leading name in quality new-age books for mind, body and spirit. Arkana encompasses the spirituality of both East and West, ancient and new, in fiction and non-fiction. A vast range of interests is covered, including Psychology and Transformation, Health, Science and Mysticism, Women's Spirituality and Astrology.

If you would like a catalogue of Arkana books, please write to:

Arkana Marketing Department
Penguin Books Ltd
27 Wright's Lane
London W8 5TZ